Practical Clojure

Luke VanderHart
Stuart Sierra

Apress®

Practical Clojure

ISBN-13 (pbk): 978-1-4302-7231-1

ISBN-13 (electronic): 978-1-4302-7230-4

9 8 7 6 5 4 3 2 1

President and Publisher: Paul Manning
Lead Editor: Michelle Lowman
Technical Reviewer: Christophe Grand
Editorial Board: Clay Andres, Steve Anglin, Mark Beckner, Ewan Buckingham, Gary Cornell, Jonathan Gennick, Jonathan Hassell, Michelle Lowman, Matthew Moodie, Duncan Parkes, Jeffrey Pepper, Frank Pohlmann, Douglas Pundick, Ben Renow-Clarke, Dominic Shakeshaft, Matt Wade, Tom Welsh
Coordinating Editors: Jim Markham, Tracy Brown
Copy Editor: Katie Stence
Compositor: Bytheway Compositors
Indexer: Julie Grady
Artist: April Milne
Cover Designer: Anna Ishchenko

Distributed to the book trade worldwide by Springer-Verlag New York, Inc., 233 Spring Street, 6th Floor, New York, NY 10013. Phone 1-800-SPRINGER, fax 201-348-4505, e-mail orders-ny@springer-sbm.com, or visit www.springeronline.com.

For information on translations, please e-mail rights@apress.com, or visit www.apress.com.

Apress and friends of ED books may be purchased in bulk for academic, corporate, or promotional use. eBook versions and licenses are also available for most titles. For more information, reference our Special Bulk Sales–eBook Licensing web page at www.apress.com/info/bulksales.

The source code for this book is available to readers at www.apress.com.

To my lovely and supportive wife

—Luke

To Mollie

—Stuart

Contents at a Glance

Contents

About the Authors

Luke VanderHart is an experienced software developer, currently working as a consultant with NuWave Solutions in the Washington, D.C. area. He has extensive experience with the Java platform, ranging from heavy data-processing applications to web development, including several different JVM languages. In addition to Clojure and functional programming, his interests are computational linguistics, the semantic web, and data visualization.

Stuart Sierra is an actor, writer, musician, and programmer in New York City. As assistant director of the Program on Law and Technology at Columbia University, he was the lead developer of the groundbreaking legal search engine AltLaw.org, one of the first production web sites using Clojure. He is the author of many popular open-source Clojure libraries, including a testing framework, I/O utilities and an HTTP client. Sometimes he blogs at stuartsierra.com.

About the Technical Reviewer

Christophe Grand is an independent software developer specializing in Clojure, Java, jQuery, web development, and all things Open Source. He is a Clojure contributor and conducts training sessions on Clojure and other languages. Christophe discovered Clojure in early 2008 while searching for a strong functional language that runs on the JVM. Clojure fit the bill perfectly. Christophe lives near Lyon, France.

Acknowledgments

Rich Hickey, for creating a brilliant new language and maintaining it with wisdom. Todd Tillinghast, who long ago taught me the beginnings of everything I know about programming. Howard Block, Rob Castle, Brad Hubbard, and Mark Keyser for being excellent, supportive employers.

Luke VanderHart

Rich Hickey, Chris Houser, Christophe Grande, and all the other brilliant people working with Clojure.

Stuart Sierra

CHAPTER 1

■■■

The Clojure Way

Clojure's Philosophy and Special Features

What is Clojure and why would someone want to learn it? At first glance, some may vote Clojure the least likely to succeed among modern programming languages, because it is new and complicated. Worst of all, it is just flat-out strange, a bewildering soup of parentheses and brackets to anyone not already familiar with the Lisp family of languages.

And yet, it is gaining popularity and momentum faster than any other new language on the market. First released to the public in fall 2007, and reaching its first stable release in May 2009, it already fosters an active, passionate community, a thriving ecosystem of libraries and tools, and is used in an increasing number of serious professional applications.

One way or another, Clojure seems to push all the right buttons. But, what are they and what makes Clojure a good choice for your project?

A Next-Generation Language

Every year, brilliant computer scientists in academic institutions around the world publish hundreds, even thousands of papers filled with new and interesting ideas. These new concepts undergo natural selection and slowly, eventually, the best and most useful of them matriculate into real-world use.

Clojure includes many of the latest and greatest of these ideas that have not yet found good (or any) implementations in other languages. The most obvious are those relating to parallel processing: Software Transactional Memory and agent-based processing are baked into the language at a fundamental level. Others (for example, persistent immutability) are more subtle design philosophies that are a synthesis of modern academic research and decades of real-world lessons.

Despite its academic credentials, Clojure's primary design goal is to remain useful and above all usable. Its advanced features are carefully selected to actually deliver to developers robust, clean code that is easy to reason and fast to write. Clojure is not an ivory tower language, but one written by a developer intended to be used in the field, every day.

Dynamic and Powerful (Yes, It's a Lisp)

Depending on your programming background, the following statement could cause either enthusiasm or mild revulsion: Clojure is a full-fledged, bona fide dialect of the venerable Lisp programming language.

Lisp has a reputation for being exceedingly powerful and expressive, and Clojure is no exception. Its functional and metaprogramming facilities make it an extremely tractable medium, malleable clay to C's stone or Java's wood. You can replace thousands of lines of code in a static language with hundreds or even dozens of lines of Clojure, with corresponding improvements in bug count and development time.

1

Boilerplate code is all but eliminated. Domain Specific Languages (DSLs) become not only easy, but the norm—Lisp programs are often written "from the ground up," evolving constructs and syntax that are most suited to the problem domain[1]. You can modify programs on the fly without recompilation or restarting.

Historically, however, Lisp also has its detractors, and many of the complaints are more than justified[2]. Lisp has suffered greatly from incomplete specifications, idiosyncratic implementations, archaic limitations, and cruft accumulated over its five decades of existence. And to many, its syntax is just too, too strange.

Clojure fixes most of these problems. It maintains Lisp's ideals and philosophy while making a clean break with the limitations of the past. It is fast, clean, and prioritizes power and elegance. Without altering Lisp's code-as-data philosophy, it provides intuitive and visually distinctive syntax that makes it much more pleasant to read than historical Lisps. After the initial learning phase, it is remarkably easy to read and write, parentheses notwithstanding.

Those who already know Lisp will immediately find themselves extremely comfortable with Clojure. To those who don't, there is no reason to be intimidated. Clojure is a clean, painless way to learn what makes people so passionate about Lisp, without having to suffer through the bad stuff. Stick with it, and it's highly probable you'll find yourself loving it, even the parenthesis, after just a few weeks of playing with the code.

The Java Platform

Whether or not you like Java as a language, the Java Virtual Machine is a superb piece of software that deserves respect. It is mature, stable, and fast. As an industry standard, there are thousands of well-tested libraries for just about any purpose. Many companies already have heavy investments in the Java platform.

By running on the JVM, Clojure immediately gains access to all of this. It is not just a port of another language to the JVM: Clojure is designed from the ground up to run within the Java environment and to easily integrate with Java. For application development, it functions equally well as a complete, stand-alone language or as an embeddable scripting tool within a larger Java program. It can be used anywhere Java can, and in most cases is much easier to write.

Functional Programming

A key characteristic of Clojure is that it is a *functional* language, which means that functions are the fundamental building-block for programs rather than instructions, as is the case in most other programming languages (known as *imperative* languages). Functional programming provides some substantial advantages over imperative programming, which will be discussed in this section. Functional style is inherent to Clojure and central to its philosophy.

---

[1] For an excellent book on the unique power of Lisp in general, read Paul Graham's *On Lisp*, `http://www.paulgraham.com/onlisp.html`, (New Jersey: Prentice Hall, 2003).
[2] See Steve Yegge's *"Lisp is Not an Acceptable Lisp,"* `http://steve-yegge.blogspot.com/2006/04/lisp-is-not-acceptable-lisp.html`, 2003.

■ **Note** Nearly all programming languages have some construct called a function. In most programming languages, the best way to think of a function is as a subroutine, a series of instructions that are grouped together for convenience. In Clojure and other functional languages, functions are best thought of as more like their counterparts in mathematics—a function is simply an operation that takes a number of parameters (also called arguments) and returns a value.

Imperative languages perform complex tasks by executing large numbers of instructions, which sequentially modify a program state until a desired result is achieved. Functional languages achieve the same goal through nested *function composition*—passing the result of one function as a parameter to the next. By composing and chaining function calls, along with recursion (a function calling itself), a functional program can express any possible task that a computer is capable of performing. An entire program can itself be viewed as a single function, defined in terms of smaller functions. The nesting structure determines the computational flow, and all the data is handled through function parameters and return values (see Figures 1-1 and 1-2).

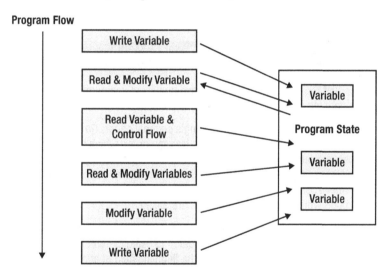

Figure 1-1. Imperative program structure

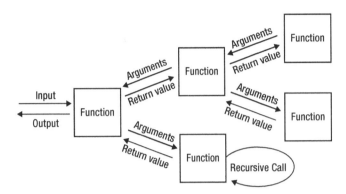

Figure 1-2. Functional program structure

Incidentally, this is the reason that Clojure code can look so strange to those unfamiliar with functional programming. It is optimized to make it easy to express function composition rather than blocks of instructions. As your experience and understanding of functional programming grows, the more natural Clojure's syntax will feel.

Equivalency of Functional and Imperative Styles

It is an important fact of computer science that the functional and imperative models of computation are formally equivalent, and therefore equally capable of expressing any computational task.

This notion dates back to the earliest days of computer science. Alan Turing's seminal paper, *On Computable Numbers* (1936) describes the abstract workings of an imperative computer, which became known as the Turing Machine. It was to become the conceptual model upon which modern computer architectures are based. Earlier that year, Alonzo Church had independently written another paper called, *An Unsolvable Problem of Elementary Number Theory*. In this paper, he created a formal system known as the lambda calculus—the formal system upon which functional languages are based.

These two ways of expressing computability were quickly recognized to be mathematically equivalent, and became known collectively as the Church-Turing thesis. This thesis, in addition to being extremely important to several fields of mathematics, became the starting point for the fledgling field of computer science.

Purely Functional Programming

Pure functions are an important concept in functional programming, as shown in Figure 1-3. Stated simply, a pure function is one that depends upon nothing but its parameters, and does nothing but return a value. If a function reads from anywhere except its parameters, it is not pure. If it changes anything in the program state (known as a *side effect*), it is not pure either.

Functional programming is largely concerned with the careful management (or elimination) of state and side effects. Both are necessary for programs to do anything useful, but are regarded as necessary evils, and functional programmers do their best to use them as little as possible.

State is any data the program stores that can possibly be changed by more than one piece of code. It is dangerous because if the code's behavior is dependent on a piece of state, it is impossible to analyze what it might do without taking into account all the possible values of that state, as well as every other part of the program that might modify that state. This problem is exponentially magnified in parallel programs, where it is not always easy to tell even what order code will execute in. It becomes nearly impossible to predict what a given state might be.

Side effects are anything a function does when it is executed, besides just returning a value. If it changes program state, writes to a hard disk, or performs any kind of IO, it has executed a side effect. Of course, side effects are necessary for a program to interact with anything, including the user. But they also make a function much more difficult to understand and to reuse in different contexts.

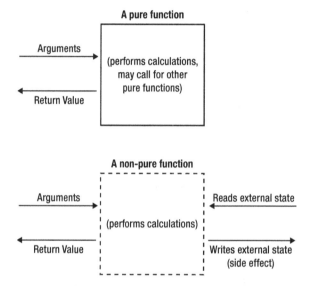

Figure 1-3. Pure and non-pure functions

Purely functions have a number of advantages:

- They are remarkably easy to parallelize. Since each function is a distinct, encapsulated unit, it does not matter if functions are run in the same process or even on the same machine.

- Pure functions lead to a high degree of code encapsulation and reusability. Each function is effectively a black box. Therefore, understand the inputs and the outputs, and you understand the function. There's no need to know or care about the implementation. Object-oriented languages try to achieve this with objects, but actually it is impossible to guarantee, because objects have their own state. An object's type and method signatures can never tell the whole story; programmers also have to account for how it manages its state and how its methods impact that state. In a complex system, this quickly grows in complexity and often the advantages of class encapsulation quickly disappear. A pure function, however, is guaranteed to be entirely described by its interface—no extra knowledge required.

- They are easier to reason about. In a purely functional program, the execution tree is very straightforward. By tracing the function call structure, you can tell exactly and entirely what the program is doing. In order to understand an imperative, stateful program you need not only to understand the code, but all of the possible permutations of state that may exist at any point in time. Purely functional code is much more transparent. In some cases, it is even possible to write tools that do automated analysis and transformations of source code, something that is next to impossible in an imperative language.

- Pure functions are very easy to write unit tests for. One of the most difficult aspects of unit testing is anticipating and accounting for all the possible combinations of state and execution paths. Pure functions have well-defined, stateless behavior that is extremely simple to test.

Clojure's Compromise

Of course, most programs can't be programmed entirely in pure functions. Side effects are inevitable. Displaying something to the screen, reading from a file on a hard disk, or sending a message over a network are all examples of side effects that cannot be dispensed with. Similarly, programs can't do entirely without state. The real world is stateful, and real-world programs need to store and manipulate data that can change over time.

In effect, Clojure does not enforce functional purity. A few languages do, such as Haskell, but they are (rightly or wrongly) considered to be academic, difficult to learn, and difficult to apply to problems found in the real world. *Clojure's goal is not to prevent programmers from using state or side effects, but to make it safe and straightforward.*

Clojure has two ways of maintaining functional purity as much as possible while still allowing a developer to easily do everything they need.

- Side effects are explicit, and the exception rather than the rule. They are simple to add, when necessary, but they stand out from the natural flow of the language. This ensures that developers are precisely aware of when and why they occur and what their precise effects are.

- All program state is contained in thread-safe structures, backed by Clojure's thoughtfully planned inventory of concurrency-mangement features. This ensures that with an absolute minimum of effort, program state is always safe and consistent. Updates to state are explicit and atomic and clearly identifiable.

Most of Clojure's unique style is emergent from these two characteristics. Very naturally, Clojure code tends to segregate itself into purely-functional and effect-producing areas, with a single function that contains side effects of manipulating state relying on other, pure functions for most of the actual processing and program logic.

This not only preserves the benefits of purely functional programming throughout most of a Clojure application, but also encourages good style. Of course, as with any other language, it is possible to write messy, obfuscated code. But more than most other languages, Clojure by its nature encourages users to write code that is easy to read and debug. Explicit state and side effects mean that it is extremely easy to read over a program and see *what* it is doing, without even needing to always understand *how*.

■ **Caution** There is a major exception to Clojure's rules about state management and side effects: Java objects. Clojure allows you to work with Java object as well as native Clojure structures, but Java objects are still Java objects and full of umanaged state. It cannot be helped. A good Clojure program will use Java objects only for interfacing with Java libraries, and therefore restrict the use of mutable state.

Immutability

One of the most important ways in which Clojure encourages purely functional style where possible is to provide a capable, high-performance set of immutable data structures.

Immutable data structures are, as their name suggests, data structures that cannot change. They are created with a specific value or contents, which remain constant over the entire life cycle of the object. This ensures that the object can be freely used in multiple places, from multiple threads, without any fear of race conditions or other conflicts. If an object is read-only, it can always be safely and immediately read from any point in the program.

This begs the obvious question: What if the program logic requires that the value of a data structure change? The answer is simple—rather than modifying the existing data structure (causing all kinds of potentially bad effects for other parts of the program that use it), the structure is *copied* with the changes in place (see Figures 1-4 and 1-5). The old object remains exactly as it was, and other threads or portions of code currently operating on it will continue to function without problems, unaware that there is a new version. Meanwhile, the code that "changed" the object uses the new object, identical to the old one except for the modifications.

This sounds as if it might be extremely inefficient, but it isn't. Because the base object is immutable, the "modified" object can share its structure except for the actual point of change. The system only needs to store the differential, not an entire copy. This property is called persistence—a data structure shares memory with the previous version of itself. There is a small computational time overhead when making a change, but the memory usage can often actually be lower. In many scenarios, objects can share large parts of their structure, increasing efficiency. Old versions of objects are maintained as long as they are used as part of a newer version (or referenced from elsewhere), and are silently garbage collected when they are no longer useful.

Original Linked List

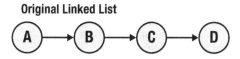

New Linked List with node inserted at head

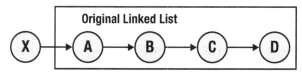

Figure 1-4. Immutable Linked List

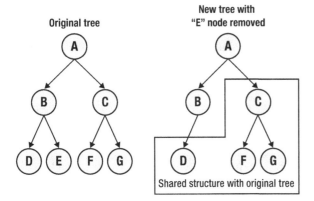

Figure 1-5. Immutable binary tree

Another interesting effect of immutable, persistent data objects is that it is easy to maintain previous versions and roll back through them as necessary. This makes it extremely easy and efficient to implement things like undo histories or backtracking algorithms.

Clojure provides the following common immutable data structures:

- *Linked lists*: These are simple, singly-linked lists that support fast traversal and insertion.

- *Vectors*: Similar to an array, vectors are indexed by integer values and support extremely fast lookup by index.

- *Hash maps*: Hash maps use hash trie datastructures to provide unordered storage for key/value pairs and support extremely fast lookups.

- *Sorted maps*: Sorted maps also provide key/value lookups, using a balanced binary tree as the underlying implementation. They are also, unsurprisingly, sorted, and provide operations for range-based access at the cost of being slightly slower than hash maps.

- *Hash and sorted sets*: Sets are groups of distinct items, similar to the mathematical concept. They support operations such as finding the union, difference, and intersection. They can be implemented as hash tries or using a binary tree with similar performance tradeoffs as the map implementations.

These objects all provide a number of other interesting features, besides immutability:

- They support fast value-based equality semantics—two data structures are equal if and only if they contain the same items.

- They implement the non-optional, read-only portion of the `java.util.*` `collection interfaces` (namely Collection, List and, Map) and `java.lang.Iterable` APIs. This means that they can be used as drop-in replacements for most of Java's collections, making it much easier to interface with Java libraries.

- They fully implement the sequence abstraction, as discussed in Chapter 5.

Clojure makes it extremely easy to work with all these data structures, and together with primitive types they provide everything a program needs for internal data storage.

What about Object-Oriented Programming?

Very clearly, Clojure is *not* object-oriented. Given how the programming world is dominated by OO paradigms and languages, many programmers will no doubt be at a loss about how to program in any other way. However, Clojure's rejection of the object-oriented philosophy is not a weakness, but rather can be a great strength, and can be leveraged to provide complex functionality while keeping code extremely simple.

For the last decade, at least, the object-oriented style has dominated computer programming through its promises of data abstraction, code reuse, encapsulation, and modularity. It has delivered on these with varying levels of success, and is no doubt an improvement over the sequential or procedural styles that preceded it. But a number of problems have also become apparent:

- An object's mutable state is unmanageable and dangerous in a highly concurrent environment.

- It doesn't really solve the problems of code abstraction and modularization. It is just as easy to write over-dependent "spaghetti" code in an object-oriented language as any other. It still takes skill and special effort to write code that can truly be used without problems in a variety of environments.

- Inheritance is fragile and can be dangerous. Increasingly, even experts in object-oriented languages are discouraging its use.

- It encourages a high degree of ceremony and code bloat. Simple functionality in Java can require several interdependent classes. Efforts to reduce close coupling through techniques like dependency injection involve even more unnecessary interfaces, configuration files, and code generation. Most of the bulk of a program is not actual program code, but defining elaborate structures to support it.

Clojure is the next evolutionary step in programming languages. It builds upon the good parts of object-oriented design, while eliminating the constraints and misfeatures that cause problems.

The notion of object orientation is not itself well defined. While usually considered a single paradigm, the object-oriented style uses a single concept—classes—to conflate a variety of actual, distinct features. Clojure isolates each of these desirable functionalities and provides separate, simpler, more powerful features to provide them separately, allowing developers to use only the features that make sense in a particular context.

- *Modularity.* Classes and packages provide a way to group code that naturally goes together and is interdependent. Clojure accomplishes this with its namespacing mechanism.

- *Polymorphism*: Inheritance and interface implementation allows common code to process objects differently depending on their type, without knowing the type or even all possible types ahead of time. Clojure multimethods provide this functionality and more—it is possible to dispatch different code based not only on type, but also on arbitrary properties.

- *Encapsulation*: Classes can be used to hide implementation details behind a common interface. As discussed, this concept is alive and well in Clojure—functions are best thought of not by what they do, but what parameters they take and what they return.

- *Reusablity*: Classes can, theoretically, be reused in different environments, put together like bricks to build up larger programs. While this usually isn't possible, it is still a worthwhile goal. Clojure also pursues this goal of modular reusability, only by composing functions instead of classes. But unlike classes, pure functions are guaranteed not to have side effects which hamper reuse.

Another major philosophical difference between Clojure and object-oriented languages is that OO languages try to unify data and behavior within classes, in some cases blurring the line between what is data and what is code structure. Properties and methods are littered throughout the code together, and completely interdependent and inseparable.

Clojure strives for a *separation* between data and behavior. The Clojure web site quotes Alan Perlis who says, "It is better to have 100 functions operate on one data structure than to have 10 functions operate on 10 data structures." Clojure tries to avoid interdependence of data on code, but instead provides a large library of functions that operate on the simple, basic data types. The important, emphasized part of a Clojure program is not the data classes and structures, but the functional code which operates upon them.

Structure of a Clojure Program

An object-oriented program consists of a set of class definitions, each of which probably contains some state, some code, and references to other classes. Programs look something like Figure 1-6.

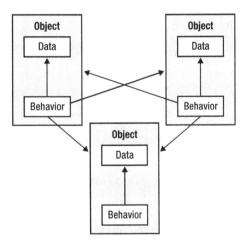

Figure 1-6. *Typical structure and data flow of an object-oriented program*

Clojure programs, on the other hand, are best thought of as a collection of functions (as befits a functional language). They are understood not by grasping the relationships between data or objects, but by understanding the flow from function to function, and the limited points where the code touches the program state. They look more like Figure 1-7.

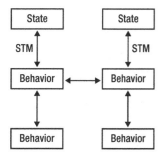

Figure 1-7. Typical structure and state flow of a Clojure program

It is worth noting that there are some problem domains, such as simulations, where an object-oriented approach is extremely natural. Clojure understands that, which is why as a language, it places more emphasis on flexibility and extensibility than any particular philosophy.

Thus, it should come as no surprise that Clojure is flexible and powerful enough to build up a custom object-oriented solution that fits the problem. It is entirely possible to use Clojure's macros and metaprogramming facilities to build an object system, completely within Clojure, and use it where appropriate. Common Lisp has something similar: CLOS, the Common Lisp Object System, built on top of Lisp macros from within Lisp. There is no reason a Clojure user could not do the same; indeed, there are several fledgling projects within the Clojure community designed to provide exactly these features.

The important fact is that Clojure *frees* you to use whatever style and structure makes sense for your project. Object-oriented systems are powerful, but they are only one tool, and the only mechanism most languages provide for abstraction and reuse. Clojure gives many *different* tools for abstraction and reuse to use where they make sense, along with the ability to build your own tools.

State Management

Nearly every program needs to maintain a working state of some kind. There will always be a need for a program to store facts and data, and update or manipulate them, from time to time.

Traditionally, programming languages deal with this problem by allowing programs direct access to memory at various levels of abstraction. Whether manipulating bytes of RAM directly in low-level languages like C or assembly or allocating objects to a garbage-collected heap as in Java or Microsoft's .NET, most programming languages are built around the concept of directly using sequential instructions to modify a shared memory space.

In this paradigm, it is entirely the responsibility of the programmer to ensure that state manipulation and access is done in a reasonable way that does not cause problems. It was never easy. Even in the simplest case, extensive use of mutable state makes programs difficult to reason about—any part of the program can change state, and it's not easy to tell where it's happening. Rich Hickey, Clojure's inventor, calls mutable, stateful objects "the new spaghetti code."

Unfortunately, with the advent of multithreaded programs, the difficult of managing state increases exponentially. Not only must a programmer understand possible program states, but they must go to great lengths to ensure that state is protected and modified in an orderly way to prevent corrupted data and race conditions. This, in turn, requires complicated locking policies—policies which there is no way of enforcing. Failure to comply with these policies does not cause obvious problems, but rather insidious bugs that often do not surface until the application is under load in a production setting, and can be nearly impossible to track down.

In general, enabling concurrency in a traditional language requires thoughtful planning, an extremely thorough grasp of execution paths and program structure, and extreme care in implementation.

Clojure provides an alternative: a fast, easy way for programmers to use as much state as they need without any extra effort to manage it, even in a highly concurrent setting. It accomplishes this through its particular philosophy of state and identity, its immutable objects, and *software transactional memory* (STM).

State and Identity

In order to understand Clojure's treatment of state, it is useful to step back and consider from an extremely high-level philosophical standpoint, what, exactly, the terms "state" and "change" even mean in the context of a running software program.

Traditionally, most programmers would say that "change" means that, given an object or data structure O, its value at a given time—call it T_1—is different from that at a later time, T_2. O is still O, whether we are looking at it, T_1, or T_2. However, some of its properties or values may be different, depending on when asked. Traditional concurrent programming is concerned with using locks and semaphores to ensure that inquires or updates regarding O's properties or values from different threads occur in an orderly way that won't cause problems.

Clojure provides a different point of view. In Clojure's world, O at T_1 and O at T_2 are not even conceptually the same object O, but two different ones: O_1 and O_2. They may have similarities in their values or properties or they may not, but the key point is that they are different system objects. What's more, they are immutable, in the strict sense of functional programming. If an additional "change" is made to O_2, for example, it doesn't result a change to the properties or values of O_2 but the creation of an entirely new object, O_3. An object itself *never changes*.

To help get a grasp on this, consider the following example. In all programming languages (as well as common sense) the number 3 is the number 3, and never any other number. If I increment 3, I get a new number, 4. I have not changed the *value* of 3, only the value of whatever variable or storage register was containing it. The notion of changing the value of "the number 3" to something other than 3 is absurd—it is hard to even imagine what it might mean, let alone the havoc it might wreak on the rest of the program which relies on the value of 3 being 3.

Clojure merely takes this intuitive notion regarding value, and extends it to larger composite values. Take, for example, a set, say "people who owe me money." Initially, the set might consist of S_1 = {Joe, Steve, Sarah}. But then I get a letter from Steve, and it has a check. He's finally paid up. People who owe me money is now S_2 = {Joe, Sarah}. These two sets are *not* the same by the definition of set equality: One contains Steve, one doesn't. S_1 is not equal to S_2 any more than 3 = 4.

Most programming languages would handle the preceding scenario by mutating the value of the set, S. In a concurrent scenario, this could cause all sorts of problems. If one thread is iterating through S while Steve is removed, it will inevitably throw an error, probably some variation of "Index out of bounds." To compensate, the programmer must manually add a system of locks to ensure that the iteration and the update occur sequentially, not at the same time, even if the code is running in different threads.

Clojure has a different philosophy. The solution is not to restrict access to S to sequential operations: that is merely a Band-Aid that does not address the real issue. The real conceptual problem is that, for a moment in time as it iterates through the set, the program assumes that {Joe, Sarah} = {Joe, Steve, Sarah}. This is obviously not true, and it is this disconnect that causes the problem. Normally, it is a reasonable expectation that an object equals itself, but not in a concurrent system that allows mutation.

By using only immutable objects, Clojure restores the guarantee that objects always equal themselves. In Clojure's system, S_1 and S_2 are different to the program, just as they are semantically and conceptually. An operation taking place on S_1 remains unaffected by the creation of S_2 and will finish without errors.

Obviously there *is* some relationship between S_1 and S_2. From a human perspective, they both represent the same concept, "the set of people who owe me money." Clojure tracks this by introducing the concept of *identity*, as distinct from value. Identity, in Clojure, is a named reference that points to an object. In the above example, there would be one identity, for example, **debtors**. At one point in time, **debtors** refers to S_1, and, at another time, is updated to refer to S_2. But this update is atomic, and therefore avoids concurrency effects like race conditions. There is no point at which the value of **debtors** is in an ambiguous state—it always refers to either S_1 or S_2, never something halfway. It is always safe to retrieve the current value of **debtors**, and it is always safe to swap its value for a new one. This is shown in Figure 1-8.

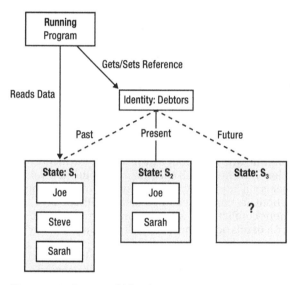

Figure 1-8. State and identity

Software Transactional Memory

A proper view of state and identity isn't the whole answer, however. Often, in a program changes to one identity depend on the state of another or a new value of an identity needs to be calculated based on the existing value without worrying that another thread will update the identity in the middle of the operation. That wouldn't cause an error, as discussed, but it might result in the results of the other calculation being inappropriately overwritten.

To accommodate these scenarios, Clojure provides software transactional memory (STM). STM works by providing an extra management layer between the program and the computer's memory. Whenever a program needs to coordinate changes to one or more identities, it wraps the exchange in a transaction, similar in concept to those used to ensure integrity in database systems. Within a transaction, the programmer can perform multiple calculations based on identities, assign them new values and then commit the changes. From the perspective of the rest of the program, transactions happen instantaneously and atomically: First the identities have one value, and then another, with no need to worry about intermediate states or inconsistent data. If two transactions conflict, one is forced to retry, starting over with new values of the identities involved. This happens automatically; the programmer just writes the code, the transaction logic is handled automatically by the STM engine.

Clojure makes the following guarantees. Transactions are always:

- *Atomic.* Either all the changes made in a transaction are committed to an identity or none are. The program will never commit some changes and not others. This provides guaranteed protection from corrupting data or creating any kind of inconsistent state.

- *Consistent.* Transactions can be validated before they are committed. Clojure provides an easy mechanism for adding run-time checks to make sure that the new value is always what it ought to be, and that there are no problems with the new value before it is assigned to an identity.

- *Isolated.* No transaction "sees" the effects of any other transaction while it is running. At the beginning of the transaction, the program takes a "snapshot" of all identities involved, which it uses for all its operations. This ensures code within transactions can be written freely, without any worry that the identities might have changed and, so to speak, swept the rug out from under the executing code.

This system ensures that there is never any blocking, and therefore, never any deadlocks. Read operations always execute immediately, returning the current value of an identity. Because the objects stored in the STM system are immutable, read operations never block a writing operation. If the read takes place and the program state changes just afterward, the object returned from the read operation does not (cannot) change, so any code using it can continue without errors. The next time the identity is read in another transaction or outside of any transaction, however, it will of course return the new value.

If one writing transaction completes while another is still underway, the STM system manages the conflict. If the two updates are on separate identities, both are committed immediately without any trouble or waiting. However, if two updating transactions conflict, they will be prioritized by the STM system, and one may be required to restart and retry. All of this occurs automatically, and without any need for special treatment by the developer.

Clojure also provides a commute operation—a writing operation which specifies that it may be performed in any order relative to other transactions. Commutative operations never block or cause retries.

The result is that the only scenario where the program cannot proceed immediately is when two write operations conflict. In all scenarios, however, data integrity is guaranteed—one of the transactions is restarted, from the beginning. Even in high-contention environments, the STM system is able to prioritize and ensure that a given transaction will almost always complete in a timely manner.

STM and Performance

No doubt, some readers will wonder to what extent this extra management layer between the program and memory impacts performance.

The answer is: very little. Because Clojure's data structures in memory are immutable, read operations have almost no overhead—they can simply pull the current value without any concern for locks or synchronization. Similarly, uncontested write operations are very fast, and only suffer a slight overhead from the STM system.

In high write-contention scenarios, Clojure's STM is probably slower than an extremely well-designed system of custom, fine-grained locks. This is an inevitable drawback of STM in general: managing transaction committal and retries adds an overhead by its very nature, and a custom concurrency solution has an advantage over a generalized one (such as STM).

Clojure's philosophy is that this slight, potential performance cost is well worth it in increased readability and conceptual purity. That efficient system of fine-grained locks is extremely difficult to get right, whereas the Clojure version can be written with almost no thought to concurrency at all.

An interesting analogy is to compare STM (managed state) with garbage collection (managed memory). It faces many of the same tradeoffs: hand-crafted, low-level code can be more efficient, but by allowing the runtime system to manage more things, the programmer's life is made so much easier. And, as technology gets better, garbage collectors have improved immensely, to the point where worrying about the few nanoseconds saved by manual memory allocation are scarcely worth worrying about. All of these comparisons hold true with STM as well. It is a tool that allows the programmer to work at a much higher level, making their job immeasurably easier. Research into STM systems is ongoing, and there is no doubt they will continue to improve and that these changes will be incorporated into Clojure.

Summary

This chapter contains a lot of dense material, and the rest of the book will be spent in unpacking it as well as showing how to actually use it in a real-world program. But the features previously outlined are truly the heart and soul of Clojure.

Understanding that Clojure is a highly dynamic, metaprogrammable dialect of Lisp will allow you to play off of Clojure's strengths, using powerful abstractions to avoid redundancy and drudgery in code.

Knowing that Clojure is a functional language that encourages functional purity when possible will help you structure your program flow in simple, elegant ways. Keeping this in mind will help you break down your tasks into discrete, small units of code, and orchestrate the flow of data between functions. You will soon come to love its immutable data structures, and the liberating experience they provide, knowing that they always safe to use.

Most of all, realizing Clojure's special relationship with persistent data structures will allow you to write robust, scalable applications with high levels of concurrency. Updating and managing data structures will become simple, allowing you to focus on the code that really matters and is fun to write, the code that gets stuff done.

CHAPTER 2

■ ■ ■

The Clojure Environment

"Hello World" in Clojure

To start programming in Clojure immediately, simply open a Clojure REPL, which stands for Read Evaluate Print Loop. The REPL is a simple yet powerful way to create programs interactively as well as interact with already running programs.

The simplest way to start the REPL is to start it directly from the system command line[1]. To do this, navigate to the system directory where you have installed Clojure, the one that contains the "clojure-1.0.0.jar" file. Then type the following to start Clojure:

```
java -jar clojure-1.0.0.jar
```

This starts up the Java virtual machine and loads the Clojure environment. As soon as the REPL comes up, you should see the following prompt:

```
user=>
```

This indicates that the REPL is ready to accept input. To write your first program, just type the following at the prompt:

```
user=> (println "Hello World")
```

Press the enter key, and the REPL should display the following:

```
Hello World
nil
user=>
```

What exactly is happening here? The acronym REPL itself gives a clue.

- *Read*: Clojure reads what you typed, **(println "Hello World")**, and parses it as a Clojure *form*, making sure it is valid Clojure syntax.

---

[1] This is the simplest way to use Clojure, but it is by no means the best. As your programs grow in size and complexity, you will almost certainly need to move to a more complete Clojure development environment that will provide help with file and classpath management, syntax highlighting, debugging, and other essential features. Plugins exist for Emacs, VI, Netbeans, Eclipse, Intellij IDEA and other editors, which provide these and a variety of other capabilities.

- *Evaluate:* Clojure compiles the provided form and evaluates it. In this case, it is a call to a build in function, **println**, with one literal parameter, "**Hello World**". Clojure executes the function, which prints "**Hello World**" to the standard system output.

- *Print:* Clojure prints the value returned from the **println** function. In this case, it is **nil**, (the same as Java's **null**, meaning the absence of any value, or "nothing"), because **println** is not a function which returns a value.

- *Loop:* Clojure returns back to the input prompt, ready for you to type in another form.

This is different from how most other programming languages work. In most languages, writing, compiling, and running programs are very distinct steps. Clojure does allow you to separate these steps, should you want to, but most Clojure programmers prefer to use the REPL to do integrated development, writing, and running their code at the same time. This can greatly speed development time. It allows developers to see what their code does instantly in the context of an already-running program without any of the overhead of the time needed to stop the program, edit the code, recompile, and start it up again. This organic, bottom-up style of coding soon starts to feel extremely natural, and returning to a static development environment soon feels slow and cumbersome.

Compared to other "scripting" languages which also provide real-time evaluation, however, Clojure's on-the-fly capabilities are much more robust. When evaluating a line in the REPL, it is not just evaluated, but actually compiled, and added to the program state of a running program on an equal footing with its pre-existing code. Nor is the REPL only a special debug feature: dynamic code is always inherent to the language. It is entirely possible, and not uncommon, to connect to a remote, production instance of Clojure, open a REPL, inspect the application state, diagnose a problem, and tweak the source code to fix a bug while the program is running for a zero-downtime code fix.

In theory, it is possible to open a REPL from scratch, and write an entire, sophisticated program from the ground up as it runs without ever stopping or restarting it.

Clojure Forms

The fundamental unit of a Clojure program is not the line, the keyword, or the class, but the form. In Clojure, a *form* is any unit of code that is can be evaluated to return a value. When you type something in the REPL, it must be a valid form and Clojure source files contain a series of forms. There are four basic varieties of forms.

Literals

Literals are forms which resolve to themselves. Examples of literals are strings, numbers, and characters that you enter directly into the code. You can verify that literals resolve to themselves by trying it out in the REPL:

```
user=> "I'm a string! "
"I'm a string!"
```

When you type a simple, double quoted string to evaluate it, the value returned is simply the string itself. The same thing is true for numbers.

```
user=> 3
3
```

Symbols

Symbols are forms which resolve to a value. They may be thought of as roughly similar to variables, although this is not technically accurate since they are not actually variable in the same way variables in most languages are. In Clojure, symbols are used to identify function arguments, and globally or locally defined values. Symbols and their resolution are discussed in more detail in the following sections.

Composite Forms

Composite forms use symmetrical parenthesis, brackets, or braces to make groups of other forms. When evaluated, their value depends on what type of form they are—brackets evaluate to a vector and braces to a map. Chapter 4 discusses these types in detail.

Of special interest here, however, are composite forms which use parenthesis. These indicate a list, and lists in Clojure, have a special meaning. It is, after all, a dialect of Lisp, which derives its name from "LIST Processing."

In Clojure (and all Lisps), lists are evaluated as function calls. When a list is evaluated, it is the same as calling a function, and the evaluated value of the form is the return value from that function. The first item in the list is the function to call, and the rest of the items are arguments to pass to the function. For example, the Clojure form `(A B C)`, when evaluated, means "call **A**, with **B** and **C** as its arguments." In other programming languages, this might be written `A(B, C)`.

This may seem very foreign to programmers without a Lisp background. However, within the context of Clojure's capabilities, the benefits are considerable. Entire programs are just lists, and lists of lists, and so on. Code is data, and data can be code. In Chapter 12, you will see how this can be leveraged to very easily create code that writes code.

Special Forms

Special forms are a particular type of composite form. For most purposes, they are used very similarly to a function call. The difference is that the first form of a special form is not a function defined somewhere, but a special system form that's built into Clojure.

Special forms are the most basic building blocks of a Clojure program, and are used to control program flow, bind vars, and define functions among other things. The important thing to remember is that, like function calls, the first form in the list identifies the special form being used and the other forms in the list are like arguments to the special form. In order to see examples each these types of forms, let's make the Hello World program a bit more complicated; you'll use two forms, instead of just one. At the REPL, type the following, and press enter:

```
user=> (def message "Hello, World!")
```

At the next prompt, type the following:

```
user=> (println message)
```

You should see the same output as the first Hello World program:

```
Hello, World
nil
```

This simple program, only two forms, contains each type of the forms previously discussed.

Analyzing the first form, `(def message "Hello, World!")` , you see first that it is enclosed in parenthesis. Therefore, it is a list, and will be evaluated as a function application or a special form. There are three items in the list: `def`, `message` and `"Hello, World!"`. The first item on the list, `def`, will be the function or special form that is called. In this case, it's a special form. But like a function, it takes two parameters—the var to define, and the value to which to bind it. Evaluating this form creates a var which establishes a binding of the value `"Hello, World!"` to the symbol `message`.

The second form `(println message)` is also a list and this time it's a normal function application. It has two component forms—each of them is a symbol. The symbol `println` resolves to the `println` function, and the symbol `message` resolves to the string `"Hello, World!"`, because of the var binding established in the previous form.

The net result, then, is the same as in the first Hello World program: the `println` function is called with an argument of `"Hello, World!"`

Writing and Running Source Files

As handy as the REPL is, in order to do any real development there is also the need to save source code and be able to run it multiple times without retyping it. Clojure, of course, provides this facility.

By convention, Clojure source code files have the extension *.clj. In a normal Clojure program, there is no need to explicitly compile your source files—they are automatically compiled as they are loaded, just like individual forms entered into the REPL. If you need to pre-compile your Clojure to standard Java *.class files, (for example, to run on a nonstandard Java environment like a mobile phone), it is entirely possible, and handled by Clojures AOT (Ahead Of Time) compilation features. These are discussed in Chapter 10.

To run the example Hello World program from a *.clj file, create a new file called "hello-world.clj" in any plain-text editor, containing the following code in Listing 2-1.

Listing 2-1. hello-world.clj

```
(def message1 "Hello, World!")
(def message2 "I'm running Clojure code from a file.")
(println message1)
(println message2)
```

There are two ways to run this file. The simplest, most often used for development, is to open up a REPL and type the following, (substituting the actual path of your *.clj file, and using forward slashes in accordance with the Java convention):

```
user=> (load-file "c:/hello-world.clj")
```

You should see the following output:

```
Hello, World!
I'm running Clojure code from a file.
nil
```

The load-file function takes a single parameter: a string representation of a file-system path. It then loads the file found at the path, and executes each form in the file sequentially, just as if it had been typed it in the REPL, and returns the return value of the last form in the file. You can see **nil**, the return value of **println** as the last line of the output. All the symbols defined in the file are still available. Try typing a symbol defined in the file at the REPL and it will resolve to the value which was bound to it:

```
user=> message1
"Hello, World!"
```

Another way to execute a Clojure file is directly from the system command line. This approach spawns a new Clojure runtime in a new instance of the Java virtual machine and then immediately loads the selected file. It is the normal method of running a Clojure program outside of development (unless you've packaged the Clojure into *.class files or a Jar package). To run a Clojure file this way, just enter the following at the command line:

```
java -jar c:/clojure-1.0.0.jar c:/hello-world.clj
```

Those familiar with Java will recognize this as a standard Java invocation. The **-jar c:/clojure-1.0.0.jar** parameter ensures that the Clojure runtime library is in the current classpath. Modify the path to reflect the actual location of your Clojure jar file that came with your Clojure installation. The last parameter is the path to the script you want to run.

This command starts the Clojure runtime, loads the **hello-world.clj file**, and sequentially evaluates each of its forms. In this case, the only results you see in the system console are those printed to the standard system output:

```
Hello, World!
I'm running Clojure code from a file.
```

Vars, Namespaces, and the Environment

As alluded to in the first chapter, a Clojure program is a living, organic entity that can evolve without needing to be shut down and rerun. This is due primarily to the existence of the REPL, and the capability it provides to evaluate forms in the context of an existing program. But how exactly does this work?

When you start a Clojure program, either by opening up a new REPL or running a source file directly, you are creating a new global *environment*. This environment lasts until the program is terminated, and contains all the information the program needs to run, including global Vars, (names bound to values). See Figure 2-1 for a diagram of what the environment looks like. Whenever you use **def** to define a Var, or define a function (covered in Chapter 3), it is added (or *interned*) to the global environment. After it is interned, it is available for reference from anywhere within the same environment. You can see this at work in the Hello World example, where you created a var binding the symbol **message** to a string value, and used it in a subsequent form.

Vars can be defined and bound to symbols using the **def** special form. It has the following syntax:

```
(def var-name var-value)
```

var-name is the name of the var to create, and **var-value** is its value. **var-value** can be any Clojure form, which will be evaluated and the resulting value bound to the var. Then, whenever the **var-name** symbol is used within the global Clojure environment, it will resolve to the var value.

■ **Caution** Be sure to define your dependencies in the proper order. Because of the way Clojure references Vars, a var *must* be defined before a symbol referring to it can be evaluated. Normally this isn't an issue, but it can result in some "gotchas" if you do a lot of work in the REPL. Because you will often define things in the REPL in a different order from how you order them in a source file, and because once they are entered in the REPL they remain available for the life of the program. As you work, you may not notice until you stop and rerun the program that you've defined a dependency out of order. It's an easy problem to fix, and, easy to avoid once you're aware of it, but it does give most beginning Clojure programmers several moments of confusion as they get errors trying to run a program that previously seemed to run just fine.

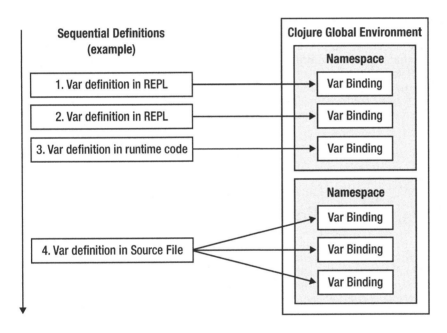

Figure 2-1. The Clojure environment

Are Vars Variables?

Although they have many similarities, Vars are not exactly like variables in other programming languages. Most importantly, once defined, they are not intended to be changed—at least, not as part of the normal running of a program. It is true, if you use **def** on a var that is already bound, its value will be changed and subsequent evaluations will resolve to the new value. However, this is not thread-safe, and **def** can only be used to define global symbols anyway. Mutable, global symbols as part of how your program works are bad news, even though you might be able to get it to run. If you need changeable values as part of your program, global or otherwise, you should always use Clojure's thread-safe reference types, *never* redefinition of symbols.

That said, there is a very good, appropriate use for redefining existing values: *manually* updating or changing a program while it is running. It is Clojure's ability to rebind a symbol that allows you to build or change a program without restarting it. It's fine to rebind symbols in the REPL, as you do exploratory programming. Another example might be that your server-based program uses a symbol to store a particular constant, say, ***max-users***, and you later decide that the system can handle more users and you ought to bump it up. In this case, it is perfectly appropriate to redefine the symbol's value without restarting the program. The key point is to not to rely on programmatic redefining of symbols to use them as mutable state. It is extremely unsafe in any scenario with multiple threads, it could be very bad for performance, and is bad Clojure practice in any case.

Symbols and Symbol Resolution

Symbols are ubiquitous in Clojure, and it is worth taking some time to understand what they really are and how they work. Broadly stated, a symbol is an identifier that resolves to a value. They can be defined either on the local level (for example, function arguments or local bindings), or globally (using Vars). Just about anything you see in Clojure code that is not either a literal or a basic syntactic character (quotes, parenthesis, braces, brackets, etc.) is probably a symbol. This covers what are often thought of as variables in other languages, but also a good deal more:

- All function names in Clojure are symbols. When a function is called as part of a composite form, it first resolves the symbol to get the function and then applies it.

- Most operators (comparison, mathematic, etc.) are symbols, which resolve to a special, built-in, optimized function. They are resolved and applied in the same way as functions with additional performance optimizations.

- Macro names are symbols. Without going into detail at this time, macros are like functions, only applied at compile-time rather than run-time. See Chapter 12 for an in-depth discussion of macros.

Symbol Names

Symbol names are case sensitive, and user-defined symbols have the following restrictions:

- May contain any alphanumeric character, and the characters *, +, !, -, _, and ?.

- • May not start with a number.

- • May contain the colon character :, but not at the beginning or end of the symbol name, and may not repeat.

According to these rules, examples of legal symbol names include **symbol-name**, **symbol_name**, **symbol123**, ***symbol***, **symbol!**, **symbol?**, and **name+symbol.** Examples of illegal symbol names would be **123symbol**, **:symbol:**, **symbol//name**, etc.

By convention, symbol names in Clojure are usually lower-case, with words separated by the dash character (-). If a symbol is a constant or global program setting, it often begins and ends with the star character (*). For example, a program might define **(def *pi* 3.14159).**

Symbol Resolution and Scope

When you use a symbol name as a form in your code, Clojure evaluates the symbol and returns the value bound to it. How this resolution happens depends on the *scope* of a symbol, and whether it is user-defined or refers to a special or built-in form.

Clojure uses the following steps in resolving symbols:

1. Clojure determines if the symbol refers to a special form. If so, it uses it accordingly.

2. Next, Clojure checks if the symbol is locally bound. Typically, local binding means it is a function argument or defined with **let** (discussed in Chapter 3). If it finds a local value, it uses it. Note that this implies that if there is a locally defined symbol and a var with the same name, evaluating the symbol name will return the value of the *local* symbol. Local symbols override Vars of the same name.

3. Clojure searches the global environment for a var with the name of the symbol, and returns the value of the var if it finds one.

4. If no value for the symbol name was found in the previous steps, Clojure returns an error: **java.lang.Exception: unable to resolve symbol <symbol> in this context (NO_SOURCE_FILE:0)**. The **NO_SOURCE_FILE** part will be replaced with an actual file name, unless you are running from the REPL.

Namespaces

When you define a var using **def**, you are establishing a global binding for that symbol name to that value. However, truly global variables and symbols have long been known to be a bad idea. In a large program, it is far too easy for definitions in one part of a program to inadvertently collide with those in another, leading to difficult, extremely hard-to-find bugs.

For this reason, Vars in Clojure are all scoped by namespace. Every Var has a namespace as a (sometimes implicit) part of its name. When using a symbol to refer to a var, you can use a forward slash before the symbol name itself to specify the namespace.

To see this, look closely at a symbol definition in the REPL.

```
user=> (def first-name "Luke")
#'user/first-name
```

```
user=> user/first-name
"Luke"
```

Notice the prompt itself: **user=>**. The string **user** in the prompt actually refers to the current namespace. If you were working in a different namespace, it would say something different. There's nothing special about the **user** namespace—it's just the default. You haven't actually just defined **first-name**, you've defined **user/first-name** which you can then use to evaluate the symbol. Since you're already in the **user** namespace, using just **first-name** will also work.

Declaring Namespaces

To declare a namespace, use the **ns** form. **ns** takes a number of parameters, some of them quite advanced. In its simplest form, you can pass it one parameter, a namespace name. If the namespaces doesn't already exist, it will create it, and set it as the current namespace. If there is already a namespace of that name, it will just switch to it as the current namespace.

```
user=> (ns new-namespace)
nil
new-namespace=>
```

Now, when you define a Var, it will be put into the **new-namespace** namespace, instead of **user**.

Referencing Namespaces

To reference a var in a different namespace, simply use its fully-qualified name. Observe the following REPL session:

```
user=> (def my-number 5)
#'user/my-number
user=> (ns other-namespace)
nil
other-namespace=> my-number
java.lang.Exception: Unable to resolve symbol: my-number in this context...
other-namespace=> user/my-number
5
```

Here you first define a var in the default **user** namespace. Then, you create a new namespace and switch to it. When you try to evaluate **my-number**, it causes an error—it can't find it in the current namespace. When you use the fully qualified name, however, it resolves the var and returns the value you originally bound to it. You can only *evaluate* Vars using fully-qualified names, though. To *define* a symbol within a namespace, you actually have to be in the namespace you want to create it in.

Sometimes, if you're depending heavily on another namespace, it's too much trouble to fully qualify every reference you need to make to a var in that namespace. For this scenario, Clojure provides the capability to make a namespace "include" another, using the **:use** parameter of **ns**. For example, to declare a namespace that imports all the symbols in Clojure's built-in XML library, you could do this:

```
user=> (ns my-namespace
           (:use clojure.xml))
my-namespace=>
```

Now, all the XML-related symbols are available in **my-namespace**. The **(:use clojure.xml)** form specifies that the **clojure.xml** namespace is to be loaded, and the symbols defined in it also imported into **my-namespace**. This is also very useful for dependency management: rather than requiring that you manually load **clojure.xml** before using it, you can use **:use** to specify it as a dependency on a namespace you declare. Clojure then loads it as part of the namespace declaration, if it wasn't already loaded, ensuring it is always available within your new namespace.

In addition to **:use**, Clojure provides another keyword you can use in **ns**, **:require.** The usage is identical to **:use**, the difference being that it only ensures the required namespaces is loaded and available—it doesn't actually import the symbols. You can also use **:require** to specify a list of namespaces to include. Here you include both Clojure's XML library and its set library at once:

```
user=> (ns my-namespace
          (:require clojure.xml
                    clojure.set))
my-namespace=>
```

Additionally, you can enclose the namespace in square brackets and use the **:as** keyword to specify a shorter alias for the namespace:

```
user=> (ns my-namespace
          (:require [clojure.xml :as xml]))
my-namespace=> xml/parse
my-namespace=> #<xml$parse_7630 clojure.xml$parse_7630@1484105>
```

Don't worry about the messy value; it's Clojure's string representation of a function, and indicates that Clojure was able to resolve the **xml/parse** symbol.

Structuring Source Files

How can you use namespaces to structure your source code and keep it organized? It is not difficult. By convention, each Clojure source file has its own namespace—a ns declaration ought to be the first form within any Clojure file. This makes it easy to manage namespaces and files. It is also similar to the Java convention of one class per file. In fact, it may be helpful for Java programmers to think of namespaces as classes. They certainly do provide ability to group relevant code together the same way classes do.

To help Clojure find namespaces when they are referenced with **:use** or **:require**, there is a particular naming convention to follow. The namespace declared in a file must match the name and location of a file within the class path. So, for example, if you have a Clojure source file at "x/y/z.clj", it ought to contain the declaration for the namespace **x.y.z.** When you reference **x.y.z,** it will know in which path and file to search for that namespace. Again, this is very similar to the Java package scheme.

Summary

This is all the knowledge that is really needed to run Clojure programs. Of course, you will want to learn some tools to help make it easier to manage and run source files. Particularly, classpaths can be painful to manage, and tools like Eclipse or Netbeans ease this burden. Another useful feature provided by most Clojure environments is the ability to open up a file, and selectively evaluate individual forms, rather than always loading the entire file. This is remarkably valuable for rapid development, testing, and debugging of existing applications.

The important fact to remember, no matter which tool you use, is that Clojure programs consist entirely of a set of forms, which are themselves either literals, special forms, symbols, or composited of other forms. Keeping this in mind is a big step towards understanding Clojure program structure.

Also, it is important to understand symbols. Symbols are the means by which identifiers in source code are linked to actual values, and it is helpful to have a clear grasp of how they are assigned and are resolved.

Vars are frequently used in conjunction with Symbols. Vars represent a binding of a name to a value in the Clojure environment, and are scoped by namespace.

Finally, on a high level, when a program gets too big for one source file break it into multiple files and give each one a separate namespace. You can then use the namespace dependency features to ensure that symbols are always defined where they are needed.

CHAPTER 3

■ ■ ■

Controlling Program Flow

Functions

As a functional language, functions are the beginning and end of every Clojure program. The "shape" of any Clojure program is like a tree, each function branching out and calling other functions. Understanding a Clojure program means understanding its functions and the patterns in which they are called. Use functions carelessly and your Clojure programs will be incomprehensible spaghetti. Use them thoughtfully and your Clojure programs will be fast, elegant, and a genuine joy both to write and to read.

First-Class Functions

In Clojure, all functions are *first-class* objects. This means the following:

- They can be dynamically created at any point during the execution of the program.

- They aren't intrinsically named, but can be bound to symbols or to more than one symbol.

- They can be stored as values in any data structure.

- They can be passed to, and returned from, other functions.

Contrast this with functions in more static languages, such as Java or C. In these languages, functions must always be defined and named up-front, before compilation. It is a tremendous advantage of Clojure (and other functional languages) to be able to define new functions on-the-fly and to store them in arbitrary data structures.

Defining Functions with fn

The most basic way to define a function is with the **fn** special form, which returns a new first-class function when evaluated. In its simplest form, it takes two arguments: a *vector* (a bracketed list) of argument symbols and an expression which will be evaluated when the function is called.

■ **Note** Vectors, delimited by left and right square brackets, have not yet been discussed. For a detailed explanation of their characteristics, see Chapter 4. For now, you can think of them as an alternate way of expressing a list. Unlike lists delimited by parentheses, they don't denote a function call when evaluated, so they are suitable for quickly and easily expressing literal data structures in code.

For example, at the REPL, you can define an extremely simple function which takes two arguments and multiplies them.

```
user=> (fn [x y] (* x y))
```

This form may look slightly complicated, but it is really very simple: it is a form consisting of just three other forms: `fn`, `[x y]` and `(* x y)`. `fn` is called with the other two as arguments—the vector `[x y]` defines that the new function has two arguments, `x` and `y`, while `(* x y)` is the body of the function, with `x` and `y` bound to their respective arguments. There is no need to use any kind of explicit return statement—the function always returns the evaluation of the provided expression.

However, this isn't much use on its own. It just returns the function, which then gets translated to a string to be printed by the REPL. The string view of a function isn't particularly pretty or useful:

```
#<user$eval__43$fn__45 user$eval__43$fn__45@ac06d4>
```

What's more, you now can't use this function, because you didn't bind it to any symbol or put it in any data structure. The JVM might have garbage collected it right away, because it was of no more use. Typically, it's more useful to bind a function to a var, like this:

```
user=> (def my-mult (fn [x y] (* x y)))
```

You can now use the new function in any context where you have access to that var:

```
user=> (my-mult 3 4)
12
```

And, it works as advertised. The expression `(fn [x y] (* x y))` is evaluated to a first-class function, which is then bound to the symbol `my-mult`. To call `my-mult`, you evaluate a list with a function as the first element. `my-mult` resolves to the new function, which is then called with 3 and 4 as arguments.

Note, however, that the assignment of the function to the symbol is only one way to use it, as long as something which resolves to a function is used as the first element of a form it will be called, whether it is a symbol or not. For example, it is entirely possible to define a function and use it within the same form:

```
user=> ((fn [x y] (* x y)) 3 4)
12
```

In this form, notice that the entire function definition, `(fn [x y] (* x y))`, is used as the first item in the form. When it is evaluated, it resolves to a function and is passed 3 and 4 as arguments, the same as when it was bound to a symbol and the symbol was evaluated.

The important thing to remember is that functions are not the same as the symbols to which they are bound. In the previous example, `my-mult` is not the function, it is only a symbol *bound* to the function. When it is called, it is not calling `my-mult`, it is *resolving* `my-mult` to obtain a function and calling that in turn.

Defining Functions with defn

Although functions are distinct from the symbols to which they may be bound, it is by far the most common case that functions are named and bound to particular symbols for later use. For this purpose, Clojure provides the **defn** form as a shortcut for defining a function and binding it to a symbol. **defn** is semantically equivalent to using **def** and **fn** together, but shorter and more convenient. It also offers the ability to add a documentation string to a function, explaining how it is used.

The **defn** form takes the following arguments: a symbol name, a documentation string (optional), a vector of arguments, and an expression for the function body. For example, the following code defines a function which squares a single argument:

```
user=> (defn sq
        "Squares the provided argument"
        [x]
        (* x x))
```

You can then call the function using the assigned name:

```
user=> (sq 5)
25
```

You can check the doc-string of any function using the built-in **doc** function, which prints information on a function (including its doc-string) to the standard system output.

```
user=> (doc sq)
--------------------
user/sq
([x])
  Squares the provided argument
nil
```

■ **Tip** The doc function is very useful for exploratory programming. All the built-in Clojure functions (as well as practically all libraries) provide good documentation, and using doc it is all easily accessible from the REPL. Make it your practice to document your functions with doc-strings as well, even if nobody else ever reads your code. You will be surprised how much of an aid it is to your own memory after a week or two. Making it easy to remember exactly what your functions do is very helpful.

Functions of Multiple Arities

Arity refers to the number of arguments that a function accepts. In Clojure, it is possible to define alternate implementation for functions based on arity.

This uses the same **fn** or **defn** forms previously discussed, but with a slight modification in the arguments. Instead of passing a single vector for arguments and expression for the implementation, you can pass multiple vector/expression pairs, each enclosed in parentheses. This is easier to demonstrate rather than explain:

```
user=> (defn square-or-multiply
        "squares a single argument, multiplies two arguments"
        ([] 0)
        ([x] (* x x))
        ([x y] (* x y)))
```

This defines a function with three alternate implementations. The first is an empty vector and will be applied when the function is called with no arguments. The implementation just returns the constant 0. The second implementation takes a single argument, and returns that argument multiplied by itself. The third implementation takes two arguments, and returns their product. This can be verified in the REPL:

```
user=> (square-or-multiply)
0
user=>(square-or-multiply 5)
25
user=>(square-or-multiply 5 2)
10
```

Functions with Variable Arguments

Often, it is necessary to have a function that takes any number of arguments. This is referred to as *variable arity*. Clojure accommodates this requirement by providing the special symbol **&** in the argument definition vector for function definitions. It works in both **fn** and **defn**.

To use it, just add a **&** and a symbol name after any normal argument definitions in your argument definition vector. When the function is called, any additional arguments will be added to a seq (similar to a list), and the seq will be bound to the provided symbol. For example, the following code:

```
user=> (defn add-arg-count
        "Returns the first argument + the number of additional arguments"
        [first & more]
        (+ first (count more)))
```

count is simply a built-in function which returns the length of a list. Try it out, using the following code:

```
user=> (add-arg-count 5)
5
user=> (add-arg-count 5 5)
6
user=> (add-arg-count 5 5 5 5 5 5)
10
```

In the first call, the single argument 5 is bound to **first**, and the empty list is bound to **more** since there are no additional arguments. **(count more)** returns 0, and so the result is simply the first argument. In the second and third calls, however, **more** is bound to the lists **(5)** and **(5 5 5 5)**, the lengths of which are 1 and 5, respectively. These are added to 5 and returned.

Chapter 4 discusses lists and some common functions for reading and extracting values from them. These will all work on the list bound to the **more** argument.

Shorthand Function Declaration

As succinct as **fn** can be when defining functions, there are still cases where it can be cumbersome to type it out in its entirety. Typically, these are cases where a function is declared and used inline, rather than bound to a top-level symbol.

Clojure provides a shorthand form for declaring a function, in the form of a reader macro. To declare a function in shorthand, use the pound sign, followed by an expression. The expression becomes the body of the function, and any percent signs in the body are interpreted as arguments to the function.

■ **Note** Reader macros are specialized, shorthand syntax and can usually be identified because they are just about the only forms in Clojure that are *not* contained by matched parenthesis, brackets, or braces. They are resolved as the first step when parsing Clojure code and are transformed into their long form before the code is actually compiled. The shorthand function form #(* %1 %2) is actually *identical* to the longer form (fn [x y] (* x y)) before it is even seen by the compiler. Reader macros are provided for a few extremely common tasks, and they can't be defined by users. The rationale behind this limitation is that overuse of reader macros makes code impossible to read unless the reader is very familiar with the macro in question. Preventing users from creating custom reader macros lowers the barriers to sharing code and helps to keep Clojure consistent as a language. Still, they can be very useful for certain extremely common forms, so Clojure provides a small set that are available by default.

For example, here is the square function implemented in shorthand:

```
user=> (def sq #(* % %))
#'user/sq
user=> (sq 5)
25
```

The percent sign implies that the function takes a single argument and is bound to the argument within the function body. To declare shorthand functions with multiple arguments, use the percent sign followed by a numeral 1 through 20:

```
user=> (def multiply #(* %1 %2))
'#user/multiply
user=> (multiply 5 3)
15
```

%1 or % refers to the first argument, **%2** to the second, etc. It can be readily seen that the shorthand function is much more compact, especially for functions declared inline:

```
user=> (#(* % %) 5)
25
```

The only downside to shorthand functions is that they can be difficult to read, so use them judiciously and only when they are very short. Also, be aware that shorthand function declarations cannot be nested.

Conditional Expressions

It is an essential characteristic of any program that it must be able to alter its behavior depending on the situation. Clojure, of course, provides a full set of simple conditional forms.

The most basic conditional form is the **if** form. It takes a test expression as its first argument. If the test expression evaluates to true, it returns the result of evaluating the second argument (the "then" clause). If the test expression evaluates to logical false (including **nil**), it evaluates and returns the third argument (the "else" clause), if one is provided, and nil if it is not. For example, the following code:

```
user=> (if (= 1 1)
          "Math still works.")
"Math still works."
```

Another example with an "else" expression:

```
user=> (if (= 1 2)
          "Math is broken!"
          "Math still works.")
"Math still works."
```

Clojure also provides an **if-not** form. This functions exactly the same way as **if**, except its behavior is reversed. It evaluates the second argument if the test expression is logically **false**, and the third only when logically **true**.

```
user=> (if-not (= 1 1)
          "Math is broken!"
          "Math still works.")
"Math still works."
```

Sometimes, it is useful to choose not just between true and false but between several different options. You could do this with nested **if**'s, but it's much cleaner to use the **cond** form. **cond** takes as its arguments any number of test/expression pairs. It evaluates the first test, and, if true, returns the result of the first expression. If the first test evaluates to false, it tries the next test expression, and so on. If none of the test expressions evaluate to true, it returns **nil**, unless you provide an **:else** keyword as the last expression, which serves as a catch-all. For an example, let's define a function that uses **cond** to comment on the weather:

```
(defn weather-judge
    "Given a temperature in degrees centigrade, comments on the weather."
    [temp]
    (cond
        (< temp 20) "It's cold"
        (> temp 25) "It's hot"
        :else   "It's comfortable"))
```

Try it out with the following code:

```
user=> (weather-judge 15)
"It's cold"
user=> (weather-judge 22)
"It's comfortable"
user=> (weather-judge 30)
"It's hot"
```

■ **Tip** cond can be useful, but be careful—large cond statements are be difficult to maintain, especially as the range of possible behaviors in your program grows. Instead, consider using polymorphic dispatch by means of multimethods, discussed in Chapter 9. Multimethods allow conditional logic, similar to cond, but are much more extensible.

Local Bindings

In a functional language, new values are obtained by function composition—nesting multiple function calls. Sometimes, however, it is necessary to assign a name to the result of a computation, both for clarity and, if the value might be used more than once, for efficiency.

Clojure provides the **let** form for this purpose. **let** allows you to specify bindings for multiple symbols, and a body expression within which those symbols will be bound. The symbols are local in scope—they are only bound *within* the body of the **let**. They are also immutable; once they are bound, they are guaranteed to refer to the same value throughout the body of the **let** and cannot be changed.

The **let** form consists of a vector of bindings and a body expression. The binding vector consists of a number of name-value pairs. For example, the following **let**-expression binds **a** to 2, **b** to 3, and then adds them:

```
user=> (let [a 2 b 3] (+ a b))
5
```

This is the simplest possible way to use **let**. However, it is fairly trivial and **let** adds more complexity than it provides value. For a more compelling example of when to use let, consider the following function:

```
(defn seconds-to-weeks
      "Converts seconds to weeks"
      [seconds]
     (/ (/ (/ (/ seconds 60) 60) 24) 7))
```

It works fine, but it's not very clear. The nested calls to the division function are a bit confusing, and although most people would be able to figure out the code without too much trouble, it is more work than it should be for this seemingly simple functionality. Also, one can easily imagine a similar function, with values and operations that are much less familiar. Such a function, written like this, might never be deciphered.

We can use **let** to clean up this definition:

```
(defn seconds-to-weeks
      "Converts seconds to weeks"
      [seconds]
      (let [minutes (/ seconds 60)
            hours (/ minutes 60)
            days (/ hours 24)
            weeks (/ days 7)]
        weeks))
```

This is longer, but you can see what's going on at each step of the calculation. You bind intermediary symbols to minutes, hours, days, and weeks, and then return weeks rather than doing the calculation all in one go. This example demonstrates mostly a stylistic choice. It makes the code clearer, but also longer. When and how to use it is up to you, but the bottom line is simple: use **let** to make your code clearer and to store the results of calculations, so you don't have to perform them multiple times.

Looping and Recursion

It will probably come as a minor shock to users of imperative programming languages that Clojure provides no direct looping syntax. Instead, like other functional languages, it uses recursion in scenarios where it is necessary to execute the same code multiple times. Because Clojure encourages the use of immutable data structures, recursion provides a much better conceptual fit than typical, imperative iteration.

Thinking recursively is one of the largest challenges coming from imperative to functional languages, but it is surprisingly powerful and elegant, and you will soon learn how to easily express any repeated computation using recursion.

Most programmers have some notion of recursion in its simplest form—a function calling itself. This is accurate, but does not carry any idea of how useful recursion can actually be or how to use it effectively and understand how it works in a variety of scenarios.

For effective recursion in Clojure (or any other functional language, for that matter), you only need to keep these guidelines in mind:

- Use a recursive function's arguments to store and modify the progress of a computation. In imperative programming languages, loops usually work by repeatedly modifying a single variable. In Clojure, there are no variables to modify. Instead, make full use of a function's arguments. Don't think about recursion as repeatedly *modifying* anything, but as a chain of function calls. Each call needs to contain all the information required for the computation to continue. Any values or results that are modified in the course of a recursive computation should be passed as arguments to the next invocation of the recursive function, so it can continue operating on them.

- Make sure the recursion has a *base case* or *base condition*. Within every recursive function, there needs to be a test to see if some goal or condition has been reached, and if it has, to finish recurring and return a value. This is similar to protecting against infinite loops in an imperative language. If there isn't a case where the code is directed to stop recurring, it never will. Obviously, this causes problems.

- • With every iteration, the recursion must make at least some progress towards the base condition. Otherwise, there is no guarantee that it would ever end. Typically, this is achieved by making some numeric value larger or smaller, and testing that it has reached a certain threshold as the base condition.

As an example, the following Clojure program uses Newton's algorithm to recursively calculate the square root of any number. It is a full, albeit small Clojure program with one main function and several helper functions that demonstrate all these features of recursion (see Listing 3-1).

Listing 3-1. Calculating Square Roots

```
(defn abs
    "Calculates the absolute value of a number"
    [n]
    (if (< n 0)
        (* -1 n)
        n))

(defn avg
    "returns the average of two arguments"
    [a b]
    (/ (+ a b) 2))

(defn good-enough?
    "Tests if a guess is close enough to the real square root"
    [number guess]
    (let [diff (- (* guess guess) number)]
        (if (< (abs diff) 0.001)
            true
            false)))

(defn sqrt
    "returns the square root of the supplied number"
    ([number] (sqrt number 1.0))
    ([number guess]
    (if (good-enough? number guess)
        guess
        (sqrt number (avg guess (/ number guess))))))
```

Let's try it out. After loading this file into the Clojure runtime, execute try the following at the REPL:

```
user=> (sqrt 25)
5.000023178253949
user=> (sqrt 10000)
100.00000025490743
```

As advertised, this code returns a number within .001 of the exact square root.

The first three methods defined in this file, **abs**, **avg**, and **good-enough?**, are straightforward helper functions. You don't need to observe them too closely at this point, unless you want to. The meat of the algorithm happens in the fourth, the **sqrt** function.

The most obvious thing about the **sqrt** function is that it has two implementations. The first can be thought of as the "public" interface. It's easy to call, and takes only a single argument: the number for which you are trying to find the square root. The second is the recursive implementation, which takes both the number and your best guess so far. The first implementation merely calls the second, with an initial guess of 1.0.

The recursive implementation itself is simple. It first checks the base condition, defined by the **good-enough?** function, which returns true if your guess is close enough to the actual square root. If the base condition is met, the function doesn't recur any more, but simply returns the guess as the answer.

If the base condition is not met, however, it continues the recursion by calling itself. It passes the guess and the number to itself as arguments, as those are all it needs to continue the calculation. This fulfills the first characteristic of recursive functions defined above.

Finally, note the expression provided as the value of **guess** for the next iteration: **(avg guess (/ number guess))**. It always passes the average of the current guess and the number divided by the current guess. The mathematical properties of square roots guarantee that this number will always be closer to the square root of the number than the previous guess. This fulfills the last requirement for a good recursive function. With each iteration, it makes progress and gets closer to the result. Each time the function is run, **guess** gets a little closer to the actual square root, and eventually it is guaranteed to get close enough that **good-enough?** can return true and the calculation will end.

As another example, Listing 3-2 is a function that uses recursion to calculate exponents.

Listing 3-2. Calculating Exponents

```
(defn power
    "Calculates a number to the power of a provided exponent."
    [number exponent]
    (if (zero? exponent)
        1
        (* number (power number (- exponent 1)))))
```

Trying it out with the following code:

```
user=> (pow 5 3)
125
```

This function uses recursion differently than the square root function. Here, you use the mathematical observation that $x^n = x * x^{(n-1)}$. This can be seen in the recursive call: the function returns the number, multiplied by the number raised to one less than the initial power. You have a base case: it checks if the exponent is zero, and if so, returns 1, since x^0 is always 1. Since you subtract 1 from the exponent on each iteration, you can be sure that you will eventually reach it (as long as you don't give the function a negative exponent). The function always makes progress towards the base condition.

░ **Note** Of course, there are easier ways to get square roots and powers than implementing these functions. Both exist in Java's standard math library, which is extremely easy to call from Clojure. These are merely presented as clean examples of recursive logic. See the chapter on Java Interoperability for instructions on how to call Java library functions.

Tail Recursion

One practical problem with recursion is that, due to the hardware limitations of physical computers, there is a limit on the number of nested functions (the size of the **stack**). On the JVM, this varies and can be quite large. On the machine on which I write this, it's about 5000. Nevertheless, no matter how large the stack size is, it does force a major issue: there is a strict limit on the number of times a function can recur. For small functions, this rarely matters. But if recursion is a generic and complete replacement for loops, it becomes an issue. There are many situations in which it is necessary to iterate or recur indefinitely.

Historically, functional languages resolve this issue through *tail-call optimization*. Tail-call optimization means that, if certain conditions are met, the compiler can optimize the recursive calls in such a way that they do *not* consume stack. Under the covers, they're implemented as iterations in the compiled machine code.

The only requirement for a recursive call to be optimized in most functional languages is that the call occurs in *tail position*. There are several formal definitions of tail position, but the easiest to remember, and the most important, is that it is *the last thing a function does before returning*. If the return value of the "outer" function is wholly delegated to the "inner" function, the call is in tail position. If the "outer" function does *anything* with the value returned from the inner function except just return it, it is not tail recursive and cannot be optimized. This makes sense when the nature of the call stack is considered; if a call is in tail position, then the program can effectively "forget" that it was called recursively at all and delegate the entire program flow to the result of the inner function. If there is additional processing to do, the compiler can't throw away the outer function. It has to keep it around in order to finish computing its result.

For example, in the preceding examples, the recursive **power** function is *not* in tail position, because it doesn't simply return the value of the recursive call, but takes it and does additional math on it before returning. This cannot be optimized.

On the other hand, the recursive call in **sqrt** *is* in tail position, because all the function does with the call is to return the value—no extra processing required.

Clojure's recur

In some functional languages, such as Scheme, tail call optimization happens automatically whenever a recursive call is in tail position. Clojure does not do this. In order to have tail recursion in Clojure, it is necessary to indicate it explicitly using the **recur** form.

To use **recur**, just call it instead of the function name whenever you want to make a recursive call. It will automatically call the containing function with tail-call optimization enabled.

For example, Listing 3-3 is non-recursive function which adds up all the numbers to a given limit, e.g., **(add-up 3)** = 1 + 2 + 3 = 6.

Listing 3-3. Adding Up Numbers without Tail Recursion

```
(defn add-up
    "adds all the numbers below a given limit"
    ([limit] (add-up limit 0 0 ))
    ([limit current sum]
        (if (< limit current)
                sum
                (add-up limit (+ 1 current) (+ current sum)))))
```

This works fine and is valid according to the rules of recursion. It passes the current number, the sum so far, and the limit as arguments. It checks for a base case (when the current number is greater than the limit), and each iteration gets closer to the base case. It works great for small and moderate values:

```
user=> (add-up 3)
6
user=> (add-up 500)
125250
```

But if you try to use it on a really large number, it chokes:

```
user=> (add-up 5000)
java.lang.StackOverflowError
```

This is where you need tail call optimization. Just redefine it, replacing the call to **adds-up** with a call to **recur**, as shown in Listing 3-4.

Listing 3-4. Adding up Numbers Correctly with Tail-recursion

```
(defn add-up
    "adds all the numbers up to a limit"
    ([limit] (add-up limit 0 0 ))
    ([limit current sum]
        (if (< limit current)
                sum
                (recur limit (+ 1 current) (+ current sum)))))
```

Now you can give it a try:

```
user=> (add-up 5000)
12502500
```

It works with no problems. Using **recur**, the only limit to how much recursion you can use is how long you are willing to wait for the processing to finish.

▪ **Note** Clojure has come under fire from some quarters for not doing tail-call optimization by default, whenever possible, without the need for the **recur** special form. Although the invention of **recur** was spurred by the limitations of the JVM that make it difficult to do automatic tail optimization, many members of the Clojure community find that having *explicit* tail recursion is much clearer and more convenient than having it implicitly assumed. With Clojure, you can tell at a glance if a function is tail recursive or not, and it's impossible to make a mistake. If something uses **recur**, it's guaranteed never to run out of stack space due to recursion. And if you try to use **recur** somewhere other than in correct tail position, the compiler will complain. You are never left wondering whether a call is actually in tail position or not.

Using loop

The **loop** special form, used in conjunction with **recur**, provides the capability to make tail recursion even simpler by providing the means to declare and call a function at the same time. Logically, **loop** is no different from defining and then immediately calling an anonymous recursive function, but it makes it much easier to "read" the logical flow and see how iterative looping and tail-recursion are actually the same thing.

To define a loop construct, use the **loop** form. It in turn takes two forms: first, a vector of initial argument bindings (in name/value pairs) and an expression for the body. Whenever **recur** is used within the body of the loop, it will recursively "call" the loop again with any passed arguments rebound to the same names as in the loop definition.

For example, the following is a very simple loop that establishes an initial binding of the symbol i to 0, recursively increments it up to ten and then returns:

```
(loop [i 0]
    (if (= i 10)
        i
        (recur (+ i 1)))))
```

Note that, like any recursive function, the loop body has a base case (when i = 10) and makes progress towards the base case with every iteration. Unlike a recursive function, however, there isn't any need to define a function by itself. **loop** sets up your functions and assigns initial values, and then provides the point that the program execution "comes back" to when **recur** is called. You can look at it equally well as a recursive call, or an iterative loop with a set of values that changes each time around.

This is extremely useful, to the point where almost all uses of **recur** in practice are coupled with a **loop.** One extremely common idiom when writing recursive functions in other functional languages is to have two versions of the function—one recursive, one not. Typically, the non-recursive version sets up some initial values and then calls the recursive function. This is a natural outcome of good recursive style—the recursive function may need a lot of arguments to keep track of its computational state, but those don't always need to be exposed to the end caller of the function. **loop** provides the capability to do this much more compactly. To see an example of this, look at the square root function introduced earlier in this chapter (modified to use **recur** instead of direct recursion).

```
(defn sqrt
    "returns the square root of the supplied number"
    ([number] (sqrt number 1.0))
    ([number guess]
    (if (good-enough? number guess)
        guess
        (recur number (avg guess (/ number guess)))))))
```

Notice the two implementations of the function—the non-recursive version sets the initial value of **guess**, and then kicks off the recursion. You can refactor this to use loop and to do both of these things in a single step:

```
(defn loop-sqrt
    "returns the square root of the supplied number"
    [number]
    (loop [guess 1.0]
        (if (good-enough? number guess)
```

```
guess
(recur (avg guess (/ number guess))))))
```

This version only has one function implementation. The loop sets the initial value of **guess** and immediately executes its body. When **recur** is called, it "calls" the loop statement again, not the top-level function. The argument to **recur** is matched up with the binding in the **loop**, so with each iteration the new guess value is bound to **guess**. The code meant to repeat is neatly packaged between **loop** and **recur**.

Deliberate Side Effects

As discussed in Chapter2, Clojure avoids side effects wherever possible, preferring a purely functional style. Some tasks, however, such as IO, explicit state management and Java interaction are, by their very nature, side effects. These cannot be incorporated into a fully functional program and so Clojure provides constructs to explicitly run side effects.

Using do

The most important and basic way to run a side effect is to use the **do** special form. **do** is very simple. It takes multiple expressions, evaluates them all and returns the value of the last one. This means that from a functional standpoint, all expressions but the last are ignored; they are present only as a means to execute side effects.

For example, take the **println** function. **println** is a side effect, since it performs output. It returns **nil**, so it doesn't fit well in a functional program (which rely heavily on meaningful return values). The following code entered at the REPL uses **do** to call several **println** functions as side effects then returns a distinct value.

```
user=> (do
          (println "hello")
          (println "from")
          (println "side effects")
                (+ 5 5))
```

The following output is produced:

```
hello
from
side effects
10
```

The first three lines are output produced as a result of calling **println**: the final value, 10, is the return value of the **do** form itself printed to the REPL as output, not a side effect. Side effects will be called whenever the **do** form is evaluated, whether at the REPL or not.

Side Effects in Function Definitions

If you have a function that needs to perform side effects, Clojure also provides a way to run side effects directly from a function definition, using either **fn** or **defn**, or directly inside the body of a **loop** without needing to explicitly use a **do** form. This is accomplished quite simply by providing multiple expressions, instead of just one, as the body of a function or loop. The last expression will be evaluated, as usual, for the return value of the function. All the other expressions are evaluated solely for side effects.

For example, here is a function definition for a function which squares a number. From a functional standpoint, it is identical to the one at the beginning of this chapter. However, it runs two side effects (specifically, calls to **println**) in addition to returning the value.

```
(defn square
    "Squares a number, with side effects."
    [x]
    (println "Squaring" x)
    (println "The return value will be" (* x x))
    (* x x))
```

As with **do**, only the last line of the function definition actually returns the value. But running the function at the REPL, you see:

```
user=> (square 5)
Squaring 5
The return value will be 25
25
```

The same construct also works for **fn**: just add additional expressions before the one that returns the value. This can be very useful, for example, for adding logging to track when functions are called.

Functional Programming Techniques

As previously described, the mechanical basics of how to declare functions and control program flow within a Clojure program. These are the basic, most fundamental components from which Clojure programs are built. Most of the rest of Clojure's standard library is expressible in terms of these basic constructs (with the exception of macro-based forms, discussed in Chapter 12).

However, to write a good Clojure program, you must not only know these forms but some of the techniques for using them effectively and understand everything that Clojure allows you to do. Most of these techniques are by no means exclusive to Clojure, but are common to all functional languages.

First-Class Functions

Functions can themselves be values and passed to and returned from other functions. This is an important feature of functional programming. It isn't just a way of doing clever tricks with code, but a key way to structure programs. By passing blocks of functionality around as functions, it is possible to write code that can be extremely generic and nearly eliminate code duplication.

There are two aspects to using first-class functions: taking them as arguments and calling them and creating and returning them. The former is somewhat more common, as it is conceptually "easier," although the latter can be extremely powerful as well.

Consuming First-Class Functions

Functions that take other functions as arguments are extremely common. These are known as *higher-order functions*. Most of the sequence manipulation library (see Chapter 5) is based around this technique.

The primary motivation for allowing a function to take other functions as arguments is to make it more generic. By delegating specific behaviors to the provided functions, the outer function can be much more general, and therefore, suitable for use in a much wider range of scenarios.

For example, the following example is a function which calculates the result of a function applied to two arguments, and also the result when the order of the arguments is reversed. The key point to notice is that it works for *any* function that takes two arguments. Perhaps you designed this function with one function in mind, but it works equally well for anything else.

```
(defn arg-switch
    "Applies the supplied function to the arguments in both possible orders. "
    [fun arg1 arg2]
    (list (fun arg1 arg2) (fun arg2 arg1)))
```

The function constructs a list of two items. The first is the result of calling the function with the parameters in the original order and the second is the result of calling them in reverse order. Test it at the REPL:

```
user=> (arg-switch / 2 3)
(2/3 3/2)
```

Here, you pass **arg-switch** three distinct parameters: the division function, the number two, and the number three. It returns a list with two items: the first is two divided by three and the second is three divided by two. Both are presented as fractions, because that is Clojure's default numerical representation for rational numbers.

arg-switch works equally well when passed other functions:

```
user=> (arg-switch > 2 3)
(false true)
```

When passed the greater-than function, it returns **(false true)**, the respective results of **(> 2 3)** and **(> 3 2)**. It works for non-numeric functions. Here you try it with the string concatenation function **str**:

```
user=> (arg-switch str "Hello" "World")
("HelloWorld" "WorldHello")
```

You can even pass it a custom function, defined inline:

```
user=> (arg-switch (fn [a b]
                          (/ a (* b b)))
```

```
                                    2 3)
(2/9 3/4)
```

As you can see, by allowing your function to take another function as an argument, you have with no extra work created an extremely generic, flexible function that can be used in a wide variety of scenarios (assuming you needed this sort of function to begin with). Defining it using a first-class function is infinitely preferable to having to write it again and again for each type of operation. When programs become more complex, this is even more of an advantage. Functions can concentrate entirely on their own logic and delegate all other operations.

Producing First-Class Functions

Not only can functions take other functions as arguments, but they can *construct* them and return them as values. This has the potential to be rather mind-bending, if not kept clean and understandable, but is also an extraordinarily powerful feature.

This is one of the main reasons Lisp has historically been associated with artificial intelligence. It was thought that functions creating other functions would allow a machine to evolve and define its own behavior. Although self-modifying programs never quite lived up to expectations, the ability to define functions on-the-fly is nevertheless extremely powerful and useful for many everyday programming tasks.

As one example, here is a very simple function that creates and returns another function which checks that a number is in a given range:

```
(defn rangechecker
    "Returns a function that determines if a number is in a provided range."
    [min max]
    (fn [num]
        (and (<= num max)
             (<= min num))))
```

To use this function, you can call it and save the result in the REPL:

```
user=> (def myrange (rangechecker 5 10))
#'user/myrange
```

Then call your new function, **myrange**, like any other function:

```
user=> (myrange 7)
true
user=> (myrange 11)
false
```

If you only needed one range check, it would probably be easier just to write it directly. But in a program where there may be dynamically generated ranges or thousands of different ranges required, creating a "function factory" function like **rangechecker** is very useful. For functions that are more complicated than just checking a range, it is a huge win, since any functions that can be generated dynamically are functions that don't have to be written manually with lots of complicated logic.

Closures

As might be gathered from its very name, closures are a central feature in Clojure. But what, exactly, is a closure? And why do they matter so much?

Briefly stated, closures are first-class functions that contain values as well as code. These values are those in scope at function declaration, preserved along with the function. Whenever a function is declared, the values locally bound to symbols it references are stored along with it. They are "closed over" (hence the name) and maintained along with the function itself. This means that they are then available for the function's entire lifespan and the function can be referred to as a closure.

For example, the -rangechecker function defined previously is actually a closure. The inner function definition refers to the min and max symbols. If these values were not closed over and made available as part of the function, they would be well out of scope by the time the function was called. Instead, the generated function carries them with it, so they are available wherever and whenever it is called.

The value of a closed-over value can't change after the function is created, so it becomes in essence a constant for that function.

One interesting property of closures is that due to their dual nature—both behavior and data—they can fulfill some roles that are assumed by objects in object-oriented languages. Just as anonymous classes with one method are used to simulate first-class functions in Java, closures can be viewed as an object with a single method. If you implement this method as a generic dispatcher for "messages" sent to the closure, it can have the beginnings of a full object system (although this is overkill for most programs). It is very common to create closures in which the data they hold is just as important as the behavior they embody.

Currying and Composing Functions

Currying, first invented by Moses Schönfinkel but named after Haskell Curry, refers to the process of transforming a function into a function with fewer arguments by wrapping it in a closure. Manipulating functions in this way is extremely useful, as it allows for the creation of new, customized functions without having to write explicit definitions for each one.

Using partial to Curry Functions

In Clojure, any function can be curried using the partial function. partial takes a function as its first argument and any number of additional arguments. It returns a function that is similar to the provided function, but with fewer arguments; it uses the additional arguments to partial instead.

For example, the multiplication function * normally takes at least two arguments to be useful. But if you need a single-argument version, you can use partial to curry it, combining it with a specific value to create a single-argument function that suits your needs:

```
user=> (def times-pi (partial * 3.14159))
#'user/times-pi
```

Now, you can call times-pi with a single argument, which it will multiply by PI:

```
user=> (times-pi 2)
6.28318
```

Notice that `(times-pi 2)` is exactly equivalent to `(* 3.14159 2)`. All you've done is to create a version of `*` with some of its parameters already defined. You could have done the same thing by manually defining a function:

```
(defn times-pi
    "Multiplies a number by PI"
    [n]
    (* 3.14159 n))
```

Although this is quite cumbersome, the entire function definition is basically a wrapper for the multiplication function, supplying specific values. This is where currying shines: it eliminates the need to explicitly write this type of simple wrapper function. The function returned by **partial** is identical to the manually defined version of **times-pi**, but by using **partial** you can leverage the fact that **times-pi** is defined exclusively in terms of the multiplication function and a particular value. This makes the code much easier to keep track of, and it mirrors the abstract logic of what is happening more accurately.

Using comp to Compose Functions

Another powerful tool to use in conjunction with currying is function composition. In one sense, every function is a composition, since all functions must use other functions in their definitions. However, it is also possible to succinctly create new functions by combining existing functions, using the **comp** function instead of specifying an actual function body.

comp takes any number of parameters: each parameter is a function. It returns a function that is the result of calling *all* of its argument functions, from right to left. Starting with the rightmost, it calls the function and passes the result as the argument to the next function and so on. Therefore, the function returned by **comp** will have the same arity as the rightmost argument to **comp**, and all the functions passed to **comp** except for the rightmost must take a single argument. The final return value is the return value of the leftmost function.

To see this in action, consider the following example entered at the REPL:

```
user=> (def my-fn (comp - *))
#'user/my-fn
```

This defines **my-fn** as a function which takes any number of arguments, multiplies them, negates them, and returns the result. Try it out using the following code:

```
user=> (my-fn 5 3)
-15
```

As expected, the result is –(5 * 3), or –15. First, the rightmost argument function is called on the parameters. In this case, it is multiplication, which returns 15. Fifteen is passed to the negation function, giving –15. Since this is the leftmost argument function, this is the return value as a whole. You can use **comp**, in this case, because the logic of **my-fn** can be expressed solely in terms of the multiplication and negation functions. Of course, it is possible to write **my-fn** out longhand:

```
(defn my-fn
    "Returns -(x * y)"
    [x y]
    (- (* x y)))
```

However, since it does nothing but compose the multiplication and negation functions anyway, it is much simpler as well as more expressive to use **comp**.

Because the functions passed to **comp** are required to take a single argument, it makes them particularly good candidates for using currying with **partial**. Say, for example, that you need a function similar to the one defined above, but that carries out an additional step: multiplying the final product by ten. In conventional mathematical notation, you want to write a function that calculates $10 * -(x * y)$.

Normally, this could not be expressed using **comp** alone—each argument to **comp** (excepting the rightmost) must take a single argument, and multiplication requires multiple arguments. But by passing the result of **partial** as one of the arguments to **comp**, you can get around this restriction:

```
user=> (def my-fn (comp (partial * 10) - *))
#'user/my-fn
user=> (my-fn 5 3)
-150
```

It works as expected. First, 3 and 5 are multiplied. That result, 15, is passed to the negation function. That result, –15, is passed to the function created by **partial**, which multiplies it by 10 and returns the final value as the result: –150.

This example should demonstrate how it is possible to use function composition and currying to create arbitrarily complex functions, as long as they are definable in terms of existing functions. Using currying and composition will make the intent of your code clear and keep things very succinct. Often, complex multiline function definitions can be replaced with a single line of composed or curried functions.

Putting It All Together

This chapter has covered the most basic elements of a Clojure program: functions, recursion, and conditional logic. To use Clojure effectively, it is very important to be completely comfortable with these constructs.

However, unlike most other languages, Clojure doesn't stop with these basic control structures. They are intended to be built upon as well as used directly. It is certainly possible to write a program of any size or complexity using just basic structures. Conditionals, loops, and function calls go a long way, and, indeed, they are the only tools available in some languages. But this can be seen as growing a program "horizontally"—piling on more and more conditions, more functions, more complex looping, or recursion. The cost of modifying or extending the program is linear; small changes or additions take a little bit of work, and big changes or additions require lots of work.

Clojure encourages you to program "vertically" by building up your own control structures on top of the provided primitives, rather than using them directly. First-class functions and closures are extremely powerful ways to do this. By recognizing patterns particular to your program or problem domain, it is possible to build your *own* controls that are far more powerful than the primitive structures could ever be. Your program can be expanded and modified with *sub-linear* effort—making small changes is still easy, but making larger changes can be easy too, since the language itself is now customized to the problem domain.

For example, it is entirely possible to do processing on a collection by recursing through it manually. But this is such a common task that Clojure has provided a powerful suite of higher-order collection-processing functions: **map**, **reduce**, **filter**, etc. These are all discussed in Chapter 5 and allow operations on collections to be expressed often with a single line rather than coding entirely new recursive functions for each occasion. The same principle applies to any domain problem. Clojure includes functions for collections, since they are used in almost every program, but you can take the same approach with problems and structures specific to any problem domain. Don't just build *out* functionality, but use higher-order functions (and later on, macros) to build *up* the tools that will help deal with that type of problem.

By the time any Clojure program reaches a certain level of complexity, if it's well designed, you should find that it looks very much like a highly customized domain specific language (DSL). This is no extra work—it comes naturally, and will actually make the program much smaller and more lightweight than using the primitive structures repeatedly. `loop`, `recur`, and `cond` are useful, but they should be the building blocks, not the substance of a program. Once a project is underway, it can be very surprising how little they are needed.

CHAPTER 4

■ ■ ■

Data in Clojure

How to Represent and Manipulate Data

Clojure is a *dynamically typed* language, which means that you never need to explicitly define the data type of symbols, functions, or arguments in your programs. However, all values still *have* a type. Strings are strings, numbers are numbers, lists are lists, etc. If you try to perform an unsupported operation on a type, it will cause an error at runtime. It is the programmer's responsibility to write code in such a way that this does not happen. This should be very natural to those with a dynamic language background, while it will no doubt take some getting used to for those who have only used static languages in the past.

Clojure types are at the same time very simple and fairly complicated. Clojure itself has only a handful of different types and as Clojure is not object-oriented it does not natively support the creation of new user-defined types. Generally, this keeps things very simple. However, Clojure does run on the Java Virtual Machine, so internally every Clojure type is also represented by a Java class or interface. Also, if you are interfacing with a Java library, you might have to pay attention to Java classes and types. Fortunately, typically the only time you need to worry about Java types in Clojure is when interacting with Java code.

Table 4-1. Clojure's Built-in Types

Type	Literal Representation	Example	Underlying Java Class/Interface
Number	The number itself	`16`	`java.lang.Number`
String	Enclose in double quotes	`"Hello!"`	`java.lang.String`
Boolean	`true` or `false`	`true`	`java.lang.Boolean`
Character	Prefix with a backslash	`\a`	`java.lang.Character`
Keyword	Prefix with a colon	`:key`	`clojure.lang.Keyword`
List	Parenthesis	`'(1 2 3)`	
Vector	Square brackets	`[1 2 3]`	

| Map | Curly braces | `{:key val :key val}` | `java.util.Map` |
| Set | Curly braces prefixed by pound sign | `#{1 2 3}` | `java.util.Set` |

Nil

The reserved symbol `nil` has a special meaning within a Clojure program: it means "nothing" or "no value." `nil` always evaluates to `false` when used in boolean expressions and is equal to nothing but itself. It may be used in place of any data type, including primitives. However, passing `nil` to most functions or operations will cause an error, since it is not a true value of any type. If it is at all possible that a value might be `nil`, you should always account for that possibility as a special case in your code to avoid performing an operation on it and seeing a `java.lang.NullPointerException` error.

    `nil` is identical to `null` in Java.

Primitive Types

Clojure provides a number of primitive types representing basic programming language constructs such as number, strings, and Boolean values.

Numbers

Clojure has very good support for numbers and numerical operations. Numeric literals can be represented in a variety of ways:

- As integers or floating-point decimals in standard notation, just type the number. For example, `42` or `3.14159`.

- Clojure also supports entering literals directly as ratios using the `/` symbol. For example, `5/8` or `3/4`. Ratios entered as literals will automatically be reduced. If you enter `4/2`, it will be stored simply as 2.

- You can enter integer literals of any base by using the form base+**r**+value. For example, `2r10` is 2 in binary, `16rFF` is 255 in hexadecimal, and you can even do things like `36r0Z` is 35 in base-36. All bases between 2 and 36 are supported.

- Clojure also supports traditional java hexadecimal and octal notation. Prefix a number with `0x` to signal a hexadecimal representation: for example, `0xFF` is also 255. Numbers which begin with a leading zero are assumed to be in octal notation.

- There are actually two ways of representing a decimal number in any computer: as a floating point and as an exact decimal value. Clojure, like Java, defaults to floating point representation, but does support exact values as well, internally using Java's `java.math.BigDecimal` class. To specify that a literal value be internally represented in exact form, append an M to the number. For example, `1.25M`. Unlike floating points, these numbers will not be rounded in operations. This makes them most appropriate for representing currencies.

■ **Caution** Because Clojure uses Java's convention that integer literals with a leading zero are parsed as numbers in base-8 (octal) notation, it will result in an error if you try to enter a literal such as **09** since it is not valid octal. Leading zeros, although mathematically insignificant, are important to indicate the way numbers are parsed.

In operations that involve different types of numbers, Clojure automatically converts the result to the most precise type involved. For example, when multiplying an integer and a floating-point number, the result will be a floating point. Division operations always return a ratio, unless one of the terms is a decimal, and then the result is converted to floating point.

There is no maximum size for numbers. Clojure automatically uses different internal representations for numbers as they get bigger and has no problem handling numbers of any size. However, be aware that in high-performance applications, you may notice a slowdown when operating on numbers larger than can be stored in the java Long datatype, i.e, numbers larger than 9,223,372,036,854,775,807. This requires a different internal representation that is not as efficient for high-speed mathematical operations, even though it is more than sufficient for most tasks.

Common Numeric Functions

These functions are provided for mathematic operations on numbers.

■ **Note** For simplicity, Clojure in its API makes no real distinction between functions and what would usually be thought of as operators in other languages. But don't worry: when the expressions are evaluated and compiled, they are replaced with optimized Java bytecode using primitive operators whenever possible. There isn't any speed lost by treating math operators as functions for simplicity.

Addition (+)

The addition function (+) takes any number of numeric arguments and returns their sum.

```
(+ 2 2)
-> 4

(+ 1 2 3)
-> 6
```

Subtraction (–)

The subtraction function (–) takes any number of numeric arguments. When given a single argument, it returns its negation. When given multiple arguments, it returns the result of subtracting all subsequent arguments from the first.

```
(- 5)
-> -5

(- 5 1)
-> 4

(- 5 2 1)
-> 2
```

Multiplication (*)

The multiplication function (*****) takes any number of numeric arguments and returns their product.

```
(* 5 5)
-> 25

(* 5 5 2)
-> 50
```

Division (/)

The division function (**/**) takes any number of numeric arguments. The first argument is considered the numerator and any number of additional argument denominators. If no denominators are supplied, the function returns 1/numerator, otherwise it returns the numerator divided by all of the denominators.

```
(/ 10)
-> 1/10

(/ 1.0 10)
-> 0.1

(/ 10 2)
-> 5

(/ 10 2 2)
-> 5/2
```

inc

The increment function (**inc**) takes a single numeric argument and returns its value + 1.

```
(inc 5)
-> 6
```

dec

The decrement function (**dec**) takes a single numeric argument and returns its value - 1.

```
(dec 5)
-> 4
```

quot

The quotient function (**quot**) takes two numeric arguments and returns the integer quotient obtained by dividing the first by the second.

```
(quot 5 2)
-> 2
```

rem

The remainder, or modulus, function (**rem**) takes two numeric arguments and returns the remainder obtained by dividing the first by the second.

```
(rem 5 2)
-> 1
```

min

The minimum function (**min**) takes any number of numeric arguments and returns the smallest.

```
(min 5 10 2)
-> 2
```

max

The maximum function (**max**) takes any number of numeric arguments and returns the largest.

```
(max 5 10 2)
-> 10
```

Equals Function (==)

The equals function (==) takes any number of numeric arguments and returns true if they are equal, else false.

```
(== 5 5.0)
-> true
```

Greater-Than Function (<)

The greater-than function (<) takes any number of numeric arguments and returns true if they are in ascending order, else false.

```
(< 5 10)
-> true
```

```
(< 5 10 9)
-> false
```

Greater-Than-or-Equals Function (<=)

The greater-than-or-equals function (<=) takes any number of numeric arguments and returns true if they are in ascending order or sequentially equal, else false.

```
(<= 5 5 10)
-> true
```

Less-Than (>)

The less-than function (>) takes any number of numeric arguments and returns true if they are in descending order, else false.

```
(> 10 5)
-> true
```

The Less-Than-or-Equals (>=)

The less-than-or-equals function (>=) takes any number of numeric arguments and returns true if they are in descending order or sequentially equal, else false.

```
(>= 10 5 5)
-> true
```

zero?

The zero test function (zero?) takes a single numeric argument and returns true if it is zero, else false.

```
(zero? 0.0)
-> true
```

pos?

The positive test function (pos?) takes a single numeric argument and returns true if it is > 0, else false.

```
(pos? 5)
-> true
```

neg?

The negative test function (**neg?**) takes a single numeric argument and returns true if it is > 0, else false.

```
(neg? -5)
-> true
```

number?

The number test function (**number?**) takes a single argument and returns true if it is a number, else false.

```
(number? 5)
-> true

(number? "hello")
-> false
```

Strings

Clojure strings are identical to Java strings, and are instances of the same java.lang.String class. They are entered as literals by enclosing them in double-quotes. If you need a double-quote character within the string, you can escape it using the backslash character, \. For example, the following is a valid string:

```
"Most programmers write a \"Hello World\" program when they learn a new language"
```

To enter a backslash character in a String, simply use two backslashes.

Common String Functions

Clojure provides some very limited string functions for convenience. For more advanced string operations, you can either use the Java string API directly (see the chapter on Java Interoperability), or the wide variety of string utility functions defined in the str-utils namespace of the clojure.contrib user library.

str

The string concatenation function (**str**) takes any number of arguments. It converts them to strings if they are not already and returns the string created by concatenating them. If passed no arguments or nil, it returns the empty string, "".

```
(str "I have " 5 " books.")
-> "I have 5 books."
```

subs

The substring function (**subs**) takes two or three arguments, the first always being a string, the second an integer offset, and the third (optional) another integer offset. It returns the substring from the first offset (inclusive) to the second (exclusive) or to the end of the string if a second offset is not supplied.

```
(subs "Hello World" 6)
-> "World"
```

```
(subs "Hello World" 0 5)
-> "Hello"
```

string?

The string test function (**string?**) takes a single argument and returns true if it is a string, else false.

```
(string? "test")
-> true
```

```
(string? 5)
-> false
```

print & println

The string printing functions (**print & println**) take any number of arguments, converts them to strings if they are not already, and prints them to the standard system output. **println** appends a newline character to the end. Both return **nil.**

Regular Expression Functions

Clojure includes several functions for dealing with regular expressions, which wrap the Java regex implementation.

re-pattern

This function (**re-pattern**) takes a single string argument and returns a regular expression pattern (an instance of **java.util.regex.Pattern**). The pattern can then be used for subsequent regular expression matches.

```
(re-pattern " [a-zA-Z]*")
-> #"[a-zA-Z]*"
```

There is also a reader macro that allows you to enter a regex pattern as a literal: just use the # symbol before a string. The resulting value is a pattern, just as if you used the **re-pattern** function. For example, the following form is identical to the preceding example:

```
#" [a-zA-Z]* "
-> #"[a-zA-Z]*"
```

re-matches

re-matches takes two arguments: a regular expression pattern and a string. It returns any regular expression matches of the pattern in the string, or nil if no matches were found. For example, the following code:

```
(re-matches #"[a-zA-Z]* " "test")
-> "test"

(re-matches #"[a-zA-Z]* " "test123")
-> nil
```

re-matcher

re-matcher takes two arguments: a regular expression pattern and a string. It returns a stateful "matcher" object, which can be supplied to most other regex functions instead of a pattern directly. Matchers are instances of **java.util.regex.Matcher.**

```
(def my-matcher (re-matcher #" [a-zA-Z]* " "test")
-> #'user/my-matcher
```

re-find

re-find takes either a pattern and a string or a single matcher. Each call returns the next regex match for the matcher, if any.

```
(re-find my-matcher)
-> "test"

(re-find my-matcher)
-> ""

(re-find my-matcher)
-> nil
```

re-groups
re-groups takes a single matcher, and returns the groups from the most recent find/match. If there are no nested groups, it returns a string of the entire match. If there are nested groups, it returns a vector of groups, with the first element being the entire (non-nested) match.

re-seq

re-seq takes a pattern and a string. It returns a lazy sequence (see Chapter 5) of successive matches of the pattern on the string, using an internal matcher.

```
(re-seq #" [a-z] " "test")
-> ("t" "e" "s" "t")
```

Boolean

Boolean values in Clojure are very simple. They use the reserved symbols `true` and `false` for literal values and implement `java.lang.Boolean` as their underlying class.

When evaluating other data types within a boolean expression, all data types (including empty strings, empty collections, and numeric zero) evaluate as true. The only thing besides actual boolean `false` values that evaluates as false is the non-value `nil.`

Common Boolean Functions

Clojure provides some Boolean functions for convenience.

not

The not function (`not`) takes a single argument. It resolves to true if it is logically false and false if it is logically true.

```
(not (== 5 5))
-> false
```

and

The **and** macro takes any number of arguments, and resolves to true if they are each logically true, else false. It is efficient in that if the first argument is false, it returns false immediately without bothering to evaluate the others.

```
(and (== 5 5) (< 1 2))
-> true
```

or

The **or** macro takes any number of arguments and resolves to true if one or more of them are logically true, else false. It is efficient in that it returns true as soon as it encounters a true argument, without bothering to evaluate the others.

```
(or (== 5 5) (== 5 4))
-> true
```

Characters

Characters are used to represent a single Unicode character. To enter a character literal, prefix with a backslash, for example, `\i` is the character "i". Any Unicode character can be entered by using a backslash, plus a 'u' character and the four-digit hexadecimal code of the Unicode character. For example, `\u00A3` is the £ symbol. Clojure also supports the following special values to make it easy to enter whitespace characters as literals: `\newline, \space` and `\tab.`

char

The character coercion function (**char**) takes a single integer argument and returns the corresponding ASCII / Unicode character.

```
(char 97)
-> \a
```

Keywords

Keywords are a special primitive data type unique to Clojure. Their primary purpose is to provide very efficient storage and equality tests. For this reason, their ideal usage is as the keys in a map data structure or other simple "tagging" functionality. As literals, they begin with a colon, for example, **:keyword.** Beyond the initial colon, they follow all the same naming rules as Symbols (see Chapter 2).

Optionally, keywords can be namespaced. The keyword **:user/foo**, for example, refers to a keyword called **foo** in the **user** namespace. Namespaced keywords can be referenced either by their fully qualified name or prefixed with two colons to look up a keyword in the current namespace (e.g., **::foo** is the same as **:user/foo** if the current namespace is **user**).

keyword

The keyword function (**keyword**) takes a single string argument, and returns a keyword of the same name. If two arguments are used, it returns a namespaced keyword.

```
(keyword "hello")
-> :hello
```

```
(keyword "foo" "bar")
-> :foo/bar
```

keyword?

The keyword test function takes a single argument and returns true if it is a keyword, else false.

```
(keyword? :hello)
-> true
```

```
        namespace
```
…·····

Collections

Clojure's collections data types are designed to efficiently fulfill nearly any need for aggregate data structures. They are optimized for efficiency and compatibility with the rest of Clojure and Java and adhere strictly to Clojure's philosophy of immutability. If any one of them is inadequate to represent a data structure, they can be combined in nearly any combination.

They all share the following properties:

- They are immutable. Once created, they can never be changed, and are therefore safe to access from any thread at any time. Operations which could be considered to "change" them actually return an entirely new immutable object with the changes in place.

- They are persistent. As far as possible, they share data structure with previous versions of themselves to conserve memory and processing time. For this reason, they are actually surprisingly fast and efficient, in some cases much more so than their mutable counterparts in other programming languages.

- They support proper equality semantics. This means that given two collections of the same type which contain the same items, they will always be evaluated as equal regardless of their instantiation or implementation details. Therefore, two collections, even if they were created at different times and different places, can still be compared meaningfully.

- They are easy to use from within Clojure. Each of them has a convenient literal representation and rich set of supporting functions that make working with them straightforward and hassle-free.

- They support interaction with Java. Each of them implements the appropriate read-only portion of the standard java.util.Collections framework. This means that, in most cases, they can be passed as-is to Java object and methods that require collections objects. Lists implement java.util.List, Maps implement java.util.Map, and Sets implement java.util.Set. Note, however, that they will throw an UnsupportedOperationException if you invoke methods which might modify them, since they remain immutable. This is in accordance with the documentation specified for the java.util.Collections interface, for collections which do not support "destructive" modifications.

- They all support the powerful Sequence abstraction for easy manipulation via functional paradigms. This capability is discussed in detail in Chapter 5.

Lists

Linked lists are important for Clojure, if only for the fact that a Clojure program itself is many nested lists. At its most basic level, a list is just a collection of items in a predefined order.

Lists can be entered in literal form by using parenthesis, and this is why Clojure code itself uses so many of them. For example, take a standard function call.

```
(println "Hello World!")
```

This is simultaneously executable code and a definition of a list. First, the Clojure reader parses it as a list, and then evaluates the list by invoking its first item (in this case **println**) as a function, and passing the rest of the parameters (**"Hello World!"**) as arguments.

To use a list literal as a data structure rather than having it be evaluated as code, just prefix it with a single quote character. This signals Clojure to parse it as a data structure, but not evaluate it as a Clojure form. For example, to define a literal list of the numbers 1 through 5 and bind it to a symbol, you could do something like this:

```
(def nums '(1 2 3 4 5))
```

> ■ **Note** The single quote character is actually shorthand for another form, called **quote**. **'(1 2 3)** and **(quote (1 2 3))** are just alternate ways of typing the same thing. **quote** (or the single quote character) can be used anywhere to prevent the Clojure parser from immediately interpreting a form. It is actually useful for a lot more than just declaring list literals, and becomes indispensable when you really start getting into metaprogramming. See Chapter 12 for a more detailed discussion of using **quote** in macros to do complex metaprogramming.

Lists are implemented as singly-linked lists and have the same performance advantages and disadvantages. Reading the first item in the list and appending an item to the head of a list are both constant-time operations, whereas accessing the Nth item of a list requires N operations. In most situations, vectors are a better choice than lists for this reason, although lists can still be useful in particular circumstances, especially when constructing Clojure code on the fly.

list

The list function (**list**) takes any number of arguments and constructs a list using them as values.

```
(list 1 2 3)
-> (1 2 3)
```

peek

The peek function (**peek**) operating on a list takes a single list as an argument and returns the first value in the list.

```
(peek '(1 2 3))
-> 1
```

pop

The pop function (**pop**) operating on a list takes a single list as an argument and returns a new list with the first item removed.

```
(pop '(1 2 3))
-> (2 3)
```

list?

The list test function (**list?**) returns true if its argument is a list, else false

```
(list? '(1 2 3))
-> true
```

Vectors

Vectors are similar to lists in that they store an ordered sequence of items. However, they differ in one important way: they support efficient, nearly constant-time access by item index. In this way, they are more like arrays than linked lists. In general, they should be preferred to lists for most applications as they have no disadvantages compared to lists and are much faster.

Vectors are represented as literals in Clojure programs by using square brackets. For example, a vector of the numbers one through five could be defined and bound to a symbol with the following code:

```
(def nums [1 2 3 4 5])
```

Vectors are functions of their indexes. This is not only a mathematical description—they are actually implemented as functions, and you can call them like a function to retrieve values. This is the easiest way to get the value at a given index: call the vector like a function, and pass the index you want to retrieve. Indexes start at 0, so to get the first item in the vector defined previously, you could do something like the following:

```
user=> (nums 0)
1
```

Attempting to access an index greater than the size of the vector will cause an error, specifically, a `java.lang.IndexOutOfBounds` exception.

vector

The vector creation function (**vector**) takes any number of arguments and constructs a new vector containing them as values.

```
(vector 1 2 3)
-> [1 2 3]
```

vec

The vector conversion function (**vec**) takes a single argument, which may be any Clojure or Java collection, and constructs a new vector containing the same items as the argument.

```
(vec '(1 2 3))
-> [1 2 3]
```

get

The get function (**get**) applied to a vector takes two arguments. The first is a vector, the second an integer index. It returns the value at the specified index or nil if there is no value at that index.

```
(get ["first" "second" "third"] 1)
-> "second"
```

peek

The peek function (**peek**) operating on a vector takes a single vector as an argument and returns the last value in the vector. This differs from peek operating on lists because of the implementation difference between lists and vectors: peek always accesses the value at the most efficient location.

```
(peek [1 2 3])
-> 3
```

vector?

The vector test function (**vector?**) takes a single argument and returns true if it is a vector, else false.

```
(vector? [1 2 3])
-> true
```

conj

The conjoin function (**conj**) takes a collection (such as a vector) as its first argument and any number of additional arguments. It returns a new vector formed by appending all additional arguments to the end of the original vector. It also works for maps and sets.

```
(conj [1 2 3] 4 5)
-> [1 2 3 4 5]
```

assoc

The vector association function (**assoc**) takes three arguments: the first a vector, the second an integer index, and the third a value. It returns a new vector with the provided value inserted at the specified index. An error is caused if the index is greater than the size of the vector.

```
(assoc [1 2 3] 1 "new value")
-> [1 "new value" 3]
```

pop

The pop function (**pop**) operating on a vector takes a single vector as an argument and returns a new vector with the last item removed. This differs from pop operating on lists because of the implementation difference between lists and vectors: pop always removes the value at the most efficient location.

```
(pop [1 2 3])
-> [1 2]
```

subvec

The sub-vector function (**subvec**) takes two or three arguments. The first is a vector, the second and third (if present) are indexes. It returns a new vector containing only the items in the original vector that were between the indexes or between the first index and the end of the vector if no second index is provided.

```
(subvec [1 2 3 4 5] 2)
-> [3 4 5]
```

```
(subvec [1 2 3 4 5] 2 4)
-> [3 4]
```

Maps

Maps are probably the most useful and versatile of Clojure's built-in collections. At heart, maps are very simple. They store a set of key-value pairs. Both keys and values can be any possible type of object, from primitives to other maps. However, keywords are particularly well suited to be map keys, and that is how they are used in most map applications.

Maps in literal form are represented by curly braces, enclosing an even number of forms. The forms are interpreted as key/value pairs. For example, the following:

```
(def my-map {:a 1 :b 2 :c 3})
```

This map definition defines a map with three keys, the keywords **:a**, **:b** and **:c**. The key **:a**, is bound to 1, **:b** is bound to 2, and **:c** to 3. Because the comma character is equivalent to whitespace in Clojure, it is often used to clarify key-value groupings without any change to the actual meaning of the map definition. The line below is exactly equivalent to the preceding one:

```
(def my-map {:a 1, :b 2, :c 3})
```

Although keywords make excellent keys for maps, there is no rule specifying that you have to use them: any value, even another collection, can be used as a key. Keywords, strings, and numbers are all commonly used as map keys.

Similarly to vectors, maps are functions of their keys (although they don't throw an exception if a key isn't found). To retrieve the value associated with a particular key, use the map as a function and pass the key as its parameter. For example, to retrieve the value associated with **:b** in the example above, just do the following:

```
user=> (my-map :b)
2
```

There are three different possible implementations of normal maps: array maps, hash maps, and sorted maps. They respectively use arrays, hashtables, and binary trees as their underlying implementations. Array maps are best for very small maps, and the comparative value of hash maps and sorted maps depends on the exact performance characteristics required.

By default, maps defined as literals are instantiated as array maps if they are very short and hash maps if they are larger. To explicitly create a map of a given type, use the **hash-map** or **sorted-map** functions:

```
user=> (hash-map :a 1, :b 2, :c 3)
{:a 1, :c 3, :b 2}

user=> (sorted-map :a 1, :b 2, :c 3)
{:a 1, :b 2, :c 3}
```

Note that the hash map does not preserve any particular key order while the sorted map sorts the values according to key value. By default, sorted-map uses the natural comparison value of the key: numeric or alphabetical, whichever is applicable.

Struct Maps

When using maps, it is frequently the case that it is necessary to generate quantities of maps which use the same set of keys. Because a normal map necessarily allocates memory for its keys as well as its values, this can lead to wasted memory when creating large numbers of similar maps.

Creating large numbers of maps is often a very useful thing to do, however, so Clojure provides Struct maps. Struct maps allow you to predefine a specific key structure, and then use it to instantiate multiple maps which conserve memory by sharing their key and lookup information. They are semantically identical to normal maps: the only difference is performance.

To define a structure, use **defstruct**: it takes a name and a number of keys. For example, the following code:

```
(defstruct person :first-name :last-name)
```

This defines a structure named **person**, with the keys :**first-name** and :**last-name**. Use the **struct-map** function to create instances of **person**:

```
(def person1 (struct-map person :first-name "Luke" :last-name "VanderHart"))
(def person2 (struct-map person :first-name "John" :last-name "Smith"))
```

person1 and **person2** are now two maps which efficiently share the same key information. But they are still maps, in all ways thus you retrieve their values in the same way and can even associate them with additional keys. Of course, additional keys don't get the same performance benefits as keys defined in the struct. The only limitation on struct maps as compared with normal maps is that you can't disassociate a struct map from one of its base keys defined in the structure. Doing so will cause an error.

Struct maps also allow you to create extremely efficient functions to access key values. Normal map key lookup is by no means slow, but by using struct accessors you can shortcut the normal key lookup process for even greater speed, appropriate for the even the most performance-intensive areas of your application.

To create a high-performance accessor to a struct map, use the **accessor** function, which takes a struct definition and a key, and returns a first class function that takes a struct-map and returns a value.

```
(def get-first-name (accessor person :first-name))
```

You can then use the newly defined **get-first-name** function to efficiently retrieve :**first-name** from a struct map. The following two statements are exactly equivalent, but the version using the accessor is faster.

```
(get-first-name person1)
(person1 :first-name)
```

In general, you shouldn't worry about using struct-maps except for performance reasons. Normal maps are fast enough for most applications and struct maps add a fair amount of complexity with no benefit except for performance. You should know about them since they will help some programs be much more efficient, but typically it is best to use normal maps first and refactor your program to use struct-maps only as an optimization.

Maps As Objects

Obviously, maps are useful in a variety of scenarios. Linking keys to values is a common task in programming. However, the usefulness of maps goes far beyond what are traditionally thought of as data structures.

The most important example is that maps can do 90 percent of what objects do in an object-oriented program. What real difference is there between named properties of an object and a key/value pair in a map? As languages like Javascript (where objects are implemented as maps) demonstrate, very little.

Good Clojure programs make heavy use of this idea of maps-as-objects. Although Clojure eschews the object-oriented mindset in general, decades of research into object- oriented design do reveal some good principles of data encapsulation and organization. By utilizing Clojure's maps in this way, it becomes possible to reap many of the benefits and lessons learned from object-oriented data structuring while avoiding its pitfalls. In the context of a Clojure program, using maps is far better, because they can be operated on in a common way without needing to define handlers for each different class of object.

assoc

The map association function (**assoc**) takes as its arguments a map and a number of sequential key-value pairs. It returns a new map with the provided values associated with their respective keys, replacing any existing values with those keys.

```
(assoc {:a 1 :b 2} :c 3)
-> {:c 3, :a 1, :b 2}

(assoc {:a 1 :b 2} :c 3 :d 4)
-> {:d 4, :c 3, :a 1, :b 2}
```

dissoc

The map disassociation function (**dissoc**) takes as its arguments a map and a number of keys. It returns a new map formed by removing the provided keys from the supplied map.

```
(dissoc {:a 1 :b 2 :c 3} :c)
-> {:a 1, :b 2}

(dissoc {:a 1 :b 2 :c 3 :d 4} :a :c)
-> {:b 2, :d 4}
```

conj

The conj function (`conj`) works with maps the same way as it does with vectors, only instead of being given individual items to append it must be given a key-value pair.

```
(conj {:a 1 :b 2 :c 3} {:d 4})
-> {:d 4, :a 1, :b 2, :c 3}
```

A vector pair as an item also works, as shown in the following code:

```
(conj {:a 1 :b 2 :c 3} [:d 4])
-> {:d 4, :a 1, :b 2, :c 3}
```

merge

The map merge function (`merge`) takes any number of arguments, each of which is a map. It returns a new map formed by combining all the keys and values of its arguments. If a key is present in more than one map, the final value will be that of the last map provided containing that key.

```
(merge {:a 1 :b 2} {:c 3 :d 4})
-> {:d 4, :c 3, :a 1, :b 2}
```

merge-with

The map merge-with function (`merge-with`) takes a first-class function as its first argument and any number of additional arguments, each of which is a map. It returns a new map formed by combining all the keys and values of the map arguments. If a key is present in more than one map, the value in the result map is the result of calling the supplied function with the values of the conflicting key as parameters.

```
(merge-with + {:a 1 :b 2} {:b 2 :c 4})
-> {:c 4, :a 1, :b 4}
```

get

The map get function (`get`) takes a map and a key as its first and second arguments, and an optional third argument specifying the value if the key is not found. It returns the value of the specified key in the map, returning nil if it is not found and there is no third argument.

```
(get {:a 1 :b 2 :c 3} :a)
-> 1
```

```
(get {:a 1 :b 2 :c 3} :d 0)
-> 0
```

contains?

The map contains function (**contains?**) takes a map and a key as arguments. It returns true if the provided key is present in the map, otherwise false. In addition to maps, it also works on vectors and sets.

```
(contains? {:a 1 :b 2 :c 3} :a)
-> true
```

map?

The map test function (**map?**) takes a single argument and returns true if it is a map, otherwise false.

```
(map? {:a 1 :b 2 :c 3})
-> true
```

keys

The map keys function (**keys**) takes a single argument, a map. It returns a list of all the keys present in the map.

```
(keys {:a 1 :b 2 :c 3})
-> (:a :b :c)
```

vals

The map vals function (**vals**) takes a single argument, a map. It returns a list of all the values in the map.

```
(vals {:a 1 :b 2 :c 3})
-> (1 2 3)
```

Sets

Sets in Clojure are closely related to the mathematical concept: they are collections of unique values and support efficient membership tests as well as common set operations such as union, intersection, and difference.

The literal syntax for a set is the pound sign accompanied by the members of the set enclosed in curly braces. For example, the following code:

```
(def languages #{:java :lisp :c++})
```

Like maps, they support any kind of object as members. For example, a similar set using strings:

```
(def languages-names #{"Java" "Lisp" "C++"})
```

The implementation of sets is very similar to maps. They can be created in both hashtable and binary tree implementations, using the **hash-set** and **sorted-set** functions:

```
(def set1 (hash-set :a :b :c))
(def set2 (sorted-set :a :b :c))
```

Also like maps, sets are functions of their members. Calling a set as a function and passing it a value will return the value if the set contains the value and nil if it doesn't.

```
(set1 :a) ;returns :a
(set1 :z) ;returns nil
```

Common Set Functions

Note that the relational set functions are not part of the default `clojure.core` namespace, but rather the `clojure.set` namespace. You will need to either reference this explicitly or else include it into your namespace using the `:use` clause in your **ns** form. See Chapter 2.

clojure.set/union

The set union function takes any number of arguments, each a set. It returns a new set containing the union of the members of the argument sets.

```
(clojure.set/union #{:a :b} #{:c :d})
-> #{:a, :c, :b, :d}
```

clojure.set/intersection

The set intersection function takes any number of arguments, each a set. It returns a new set containing the intersection of the members of the argument sets or the empty set if there is no intersection.

```
(clojure.set/intersection #{:a :b :c :d} #{:c :d :f :g})
-> #{:c, :d}
```

clojure.set/difference

The set difference function takes any number of arguments, each a set. It returns a new set containing the members of the first set without the members of the remaining sets.

```
(clojure.set/difference #{:a :b :c :d} #{:c :d})
-> #{:a, :b}
```

Summary

Clojure provides a very complete and capable set of data types which in combination should be able to meet just about any programming need. Its primitive types provide the basic building blocks of any program, including very rich, worry-free numeric and string support.

The true strength of Clojure's data system, however, lies in its collections library. Collections are important not just convenient things to use, but are integral to Clojure's philosophy on data and immutability. They strictly adhere to the principles of immutability, meaning they cannot be changed, and persistence, meaning they share their structure for maximum efficiency. Relying on Clojure's built-in data structures and being familiar with the methods available for them will go a long way towards making your code efficient, readable, and idiomatic.

CHAPTER 5

■ ■ ■

Sequences

What Are Sequences?

In Clojure, sequences are a unified way to read, write, and modify any data structure that is logically a collection of items. They are built into Clojure at a very basic level, and are by far the most convenient and idiomatic way to handle collections. They fill the role occupied by lists in other Lisp dialects. More than just a collection API, they are the framework around which program flow and logic are often constructed, and are designed to be as easy-to-use as the basis for recursion and higher-order function application.

Fundamentally, sequences are an abstraction, a common programming interface that generalizes behavior common to all collections and exposes it via a library of *sequence functions*. Sequences are a result of the observation that the classic operations on linked lists, such as "first" and "rest" (or "car" and "cdr", for those with a lisp background) and work equally well on just about any data type. For example, the first function returns the first item in a sequence. Whether the sequence is actually a list, vector, set, or even a map doesn't matter.

```
user=> (def mylist '(1 2 3))
user=> (first mylist)
1

user=> (def myvec [1 2 3])
user=> (first myvec)
1

user=> (def myset #{1 2 3})
user=> (first myset)
1

user=> (def mymap {:a 1 :b 2 :c 3})
user=> (first mymap)
[:a 1]
```

Similarly, the rest function operates on any sequence, returning a sequence of everything except the first item:

```
user=> (def mylist '(1 2 3))
user=> (rest mylist)
(2 3)
```

Sequence functions are extremely useful. For example, with just first and rest (and another function, empty?, which returns true if a sequence is empty) it is possible to implement a very common Lisp idiom: a function that recurses over a list. However, because you're using sequences, it doesn't have to be a list—it can be any collection.

```
(defn printall [s]
    (if (not (empty? s))
        (do
            (println (str "Item: " (first s)))
            (recur (rest s)))))
```

This function takes a sequence, and checks that it is not empty. If it is empty, it does nothing (implicitly returns nil). If it has items, it prints a string as a side effect, printing "Item:" concatenated with the first item in the sequence. It then recurses, passing the rest of the sequence to the next iteration. It works on lists:

```
user=> (printall '(1 2 3))
Item: 1
Item: 2
Item: 3
nil
```

And on vectors:

```
user=> (printall ["vector" "of" "strings"])
Item: vector
Item: of
Item: strings
nil
```

And even on strings, which happen to be sequences of characters:

```
user=> (printall " Hello")
Item: H
Item: e
Item: l
Item: l
Item: o
nil
```

Because sequences are so generic, the same function works perfectly well for all these disparate collection types.

■ **Caution** Technically, the various types of data structure are not sequences themselves, but rather can be turned *into* sequences with the `seq` function. `seq` takes a single argument and creates a sequence view of it. For example, a vector is not a sequence, but the result of (`seq any-vector`) is. Since almost all the sequence functions call `seq` on their arguments internally, there isn't much distinction in practice most of the time. Be aware of this, however, in case you run across a function that actually requires a sequence, not a collection that is sequence-able: there is a difference. You can just call `seq` on any collection to efficiently retrieve a sequence view of it.

Sequenceable Types

Sequences can be created from nearly any backing collection type.

- *Clojure's persistent collections*: Maps, sets, lists, and vectors all work nicely as sequences.

- *Strings*: All strings are sequences of characters.

- *Java arrays*: This can result in a mismatch, however, since Java arrays are mutable and sequences are not to avoid difficult bugs, avoid modifying arrays while you are using a sequence based on them.

- *Any Java collection which implements the java.lang.Iterable interface*: Again, however, Java collections are mutable whereas sequences are not, so avoid modifying a collection while using a sequence view of it.

- *Natively*: Sequences can also be constructed directly without being backed by another collection type.

Anatomy of a Sequence

It is important to understand the underlying logical structure of a sequence. Sequences that were created in different ways have widely differing implementations. A sequence representation of a vector, for example, is still a vector under the hood, with the same performance characteristics. But all sequences share the same conceptual model: a singly-linked list implemented in terms of `first` and `rest`. `first` and `rest`, incidentally, are identical to `car` and `cdr` in traditional Lisps. They were renamed to more accurately reflect their intent in terms familiar to modern programmers.

Every sequence, conceptually, consists of these two parts: the first item in the sequence, accessed by the `first` function, and another sequence representing all the rest of the items, accessed by the `rest` function. Each sequence of *n* items is actually comprised of *n*-1 component sequences. The sequence ends when `rest` returns empty. All other sequence functions can be defined in terms of `first` and `rest`, although sequences created from collection types implement them directly for better performance.

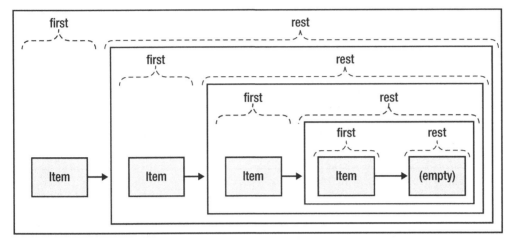

Figure 5-1. Sequence illustration, showing component sequences

Constructing Sequences

Using this model of sequences, it is easy to construct them directly using either the cons or conj functions. The cons function stands for "construct" and takes two arguments, an item and a sequence. It returns a new sequence created using the item as its first and the sequence as its rest. A sequence created by cons is known as a "cons cell"—a simple first/rest pair. Sequences of any length can be constructed by chaining together multiple cons cells.

```
user=> (cons 4 '(1 2 3))
(4 1 2 3)
```

The conj function is similar to cons and stands for "conjoin." The main difference from cons is that (if possible) it reuses the underlying implementation of the sequence instead of always creating a cons cell. This usually results in sequences that are more efficient. Whether the new item is appended to the beginning or end depends on the underlying representation of the sequence. Unlike cons, conj takes a sequence as its first parameter, and the item to append as the second:

```
user=> (conj '(1 2 3) 4)
(4 1 2 3)
```

conj also supports adding any number of items at once: just use additional parameters. The parameters are appended to the front of the sequence in the order they are provided.

```
user=> (conj '(1 2 3) 4 5 6)
(6 5 4 1 2 3)
```

■ **Caution** A feature of `conj` you should take note of is that it doesn't call `seq` on its argument. It can work on data structures directly as well as sequences. In this case, it adds the new item wherever it's most efficient, not necessarily at the front (as it does with sequences). With vectors, for example, the most efficient place to add items is the end. So (`conj [1 2] 3`) yields [1 2 3], not [3 1 2]. If you know you want a sequence, and you want the added item at the front, call `seq` on the vector first: (`conj (seq [1 2]) 3`) yields (3 1 2) as expected. You could also just use `cons` instead. Use `conj` when you don't want to convert your collection to a sequence.

For both `conj` and `cons`, if you supply `nil` in place of the sequence, it constructs a sequence containing only one item, the one you specified.

```
user=> (cons 1 nil)
(1)
```

This is used in another common Lisp idiom, constructing a list recursively using cons or conj. The following function demonstrates recursively constructing a sequence of all the integers from 1 to the provided parameter:

```
(defn make-int-seq [max]
    (loop [acc nil n max]
        (if (zero? n)
            acc
            (recur (cons n acc) (dec n)))))
```

With each iteration, this function conses the value of n (initially the maximum value) to an accumulator sequence argument (initially nil), and then recurses, passing the new accumulator and the new decremented value of n. When n reaches zero, the function simply returns the accumulator, which at that point contains all the integers from 1 to the maximum.

```
user=> (make-int-seq 5)
(1 2 3 4 5)
```

Lazy Sequences

The first/rest architecture of sequences is the basis for another extremely important aspect of Clojure sequences: laziness. Lazy sequences provide a conceptually simple and highly efficient way to operate on amounts of data too large to fit in system memory at once. They can be infinitely long, but still can be utilized efficiently by any standard sequence function. As a high-level abstraction, they allow the developer to focus on the computation being performed, rather than managing the ins and outs of loading or creating data.

Laziness is made possible by the observation that logically, the rest of a sequence doesn't need to actually exist, provided it can be created when necessary. Rather than containing an actual, concrete series of values, the rest of a lazy sequence can be implemented as a function which *returns* a sequence. From the perspective of functions using the sequence, there is no difference; when they call the rest function, they get a sequence. The difference is that in the case of a normal sequence, it is returning a data structure that already existed in memory. In a lazy sequence, calling rest actually calculates and instantiates the new sequence, with a freshly calculated value for its first and updated instructions on how to generate still *more* values as its rest.

For efficiency, once a lazy sequence is realized, the value is cached as a normal, non-lazy sequence—subsequent accesses to the sequence are handled normally, rather than being lazily generated. This ensures that the calculation needed to generate it is only called once: using large, "heavyweight" calculations as generators in lazy sequences pose no problem, since they are guaranteed not to be executed more than once. The cached values are stored as long as there is code using them. When no references remain, the cached sequence is garbage collected like any other object.

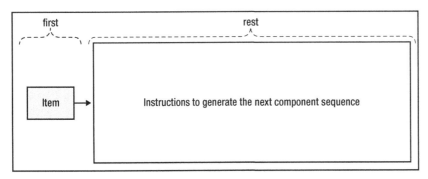

Figure 5-2. *Lazy sequences*

An Example of Laziness

To see a lazy sequence at work, consider the map function. The map function is an extremely important sequence manipulation tool in Clojure. It works by taking a sequence and a function as arguments, and returns a new sequence which is the result of applying the supplied function to each of the values in the original sequence. For example, if you run map with the sequence '(1 2 3 4 5 6 7) and a function which squares its parameter, (fn [x] (*x x)), the return value of map will be '(1 4 9 16 25 36 49). This is the sequence formed by squaring each of the values in the original sequence.

```
user => (map
            (fn [x] (* x x))
                '(1 2 3 4 5 6 7))
(1 4 9 16 25 36 49)
```

What is not immediately apparent is that the return value of map is actually always a lazy sequence. Since the return value is immediately printed to the REPL anyway, the difference is transparent—the actual values are immediately realized.

To see the internal workings of the lazy sequence, let's add a side effect to your square function, so you can see when it's being executed (normally, side effects in functions provided to map are not a great design practice, but here they will provide insight into how lazy sequences work). In your new square function, you will now print out the value of each parameter as it is processed. To make things simpler, you'll use defn to define it rather than inlining it in the call to map:

```
(defn square [x]
    (do
```

```
(println (str "Processing: " x))
(* x x)))
```

This function is exactly the same as the previous version, except that it uses do to run an explicit side effect, printing out the value of each parameter as it is processed. Running it returns this rather surprising and somewhat messy result:

```
user => (map square '(1 2 3 4 5)
(Processing:1
Processing:2
1 Processing:3
4 Processing:4
9 Processing:5
16 25)
```

The reason why the code is so ugly is that the println calls are being called in the *middle* of printing out the results. The square function (containing println call) is not being called until it is absolutely required—until the system is actually ready to realize the lazy values. So your tracing statements from println and the actual output of the function, "(1 4 9 16 25)", are all mixed up.

To make this even clearer, let's bind the result of the map call to a symbol:

```
user =>(def map-result (map square '(1 2 3 4 5))
#'user/map-result
```

You now have a symbol map-result which is, supposedly, bound to a sequence of the squares. However, you didn't see the trace statement. square was never actually called! map-result is a lazy sequence. Logically, it does contain the squares you expected, but they haven't been realized yet. It's not a sequence of squares, but a *promise* of a sequence of squares. You can pass it all around the program, or store it, and the actual work of calculating the squares is deferred until it is required.

Now, let's retrieve some of its values using the nth function, which retrieves the value at a certain index of a sequence. Calling (nth map-result 2) should return 9, since 3 squared is 9, and 3 was the 2nd item in the original sequence (counting from 0 becauseall indexes in Clojure start at 0).

```
user => (nth map-result 2)
Processing:1
Processing:2
Processing:3
9
```

You can see from the trace statements that the square function was called three times—just enough to calculate the third value in the sequence. Making the exact same call again, however, does not call the square function:

```
user => (nth map-result 2)
9
```

The values were already cached, so there was no need to call square to calculate them again. Now, printing the value of the whole sequence:

```
user => (println map-result)
(1 4 Processing:4
```

```
9 Processing:5
16 25)
```

It only calls square twice, for the two remaining unrealized values in the lazy sequence. The cached values are not recalculated.

This example shows how the lazy sequence returned by map defers the actual calculation of its values until they are absolutely required.

Constructing Lazy Sequences

Obtaining a lazy sequence is easy. Most of Clojure's built-in sequence functions such as map and filter return lazy sequences by default. If you want to generate your own lazy sequences, there are two ways to do so: constructing it directly or using a function that generates a lazy sequence for you.

Constructing Lazy Sequences Directly

To build a lazy sequence manually, use the built-in lazy-seq macro to wrap code that would otherwise return a normal sequence. lazy-seq builds a lazy sequence with any code it contains as a deferred value. Code wrapped in lazy-seq is not executed immediately, but "saved for later" within the context of a lazy sequence.

For example, the following function generates an infinite lazy sequence formed by taking a base, and then successively adding a number to it.

```
(defn lazy-counter [base increment]
    (lazy-seq
        (cons base (lazy-counter (+ base increment) increment))))
```

Then, you can call the function, and use the take function to get the first several values of the lazy sequence. (take has two arguments, a number and a collection. It returns a sequence obtained by taking the number of elements from the collection.)

```
user=> (take 10 (lazy-counter 0 2))
(0 2 4 6 8 10 12 14 16 18)
```

The sequence, logically, is truly infinite. For example, to get the millionth number, counting by 3 starting from 2, just use nth:

```
user=> (nth (lazy-counter 2 3) 1000000)
3000002
```

Because it is infinite, you can use lazy-counter to get a sequence of *any* length—the only limitation will be how long it takes the computer to count up to a million, a billion, or whatever number you choose.

Compare this to a non-lazy version:

```
(defn counter [base increment]
        (cons base (counter (+ base increment) increment)))
```

This function doesn't even make it off the ground. It crashes with a StackOverflowError almost immediately. Because it doesn't defer any execution, it immediately recurses until it uses up all the stack space in the JVM. The lazy version doesn't have this problem. Although it is defined recursively, the contents of lazy-seq are only called when the internal code that processes lazy sequences is ready to unfold the next value. This is done in a way which does not consume stack space, and so lazy sequences are effective as well as logically infinite.

■ **Caution** Be careful with infinite sequences. They are logically infinite, but care is required not to attempt to realize an infinite number of values. Trying to print an infinite lazy sequence in the REPL directly, for example, without using take or an equivalent can lock the program as it churns through the lazy sequence, on to infinity, without stopping. In this and other common scenarios, it is still possible to write code that will continue processing an infinite sequence forever, locking up the thread in which it is running. Infinite sequences can be very useful, but make sure code that utilizes them has proper exit conditions and doesn't depend on hitting the end of the sequence. Just because the sequence is infinite doesn't mean you want to take an infinite amount of time to process it, or try to load the whole thing into memory at once. Sadly, computers are finite machines.

Constructing Lazy Sequences Using Sequence Generator Functions

For many common cases where a lazy sequence is required, it's often easier to use a sequence generator function than lazy-seq directly. In particular, iterate is useful. It generates an infinite sequence of items by calling a supplied function, passing the previous item as an argument. It takes two arguments: the function to call and an initial value for the first item in the sequence.

For example, to generate an infinite lazy sequence of all the integers use iterate with the built-in increment function, inc:

```
user=> (def integers (iterate inc 0))
#'user/integers
user=> (take 10 integers)
(0 1 2 3 4 5 6 7 8 9)
```

By providing a custom function, iterate can also be used to provide functionality identical to the lazy-counter function defined above:

```
(defn lazy-counter-iterate [base increment]
      (iterate (fn [n] (+ n increment)) base))
```

```
user=> (nth (lazy-counter-iterate 2 3) 1000000)
3000002
```

There are several other functions that generate sequences similarly to iterate: see the section "The Sequence API."

Lazy Sequences and Memory Management

It is important to understand how lazy sequences consume memory. It is possible to use large, even infinite sequences in a memory-efficient way, but unfortunately it is also possible to inadvertently consume large amounts of memory, even resulting in a Java `OutOfMemoryError` if they exceed the available heap space in the JVM instance.

Use the following guidelines to reason about how lazy sequences consume memory:

- Lazy sequences which have not yet been realized consume no appreciable memory (other than the few bytes used to contain their definition).

- Once a lazy sequence is realized, it will consume memory for all the values it contains, *provided there is a reference to the realized sequence,* until the reference to the realized sequence is discarded and the sequence is garbage collected.

The final distinction is key. To illustrate the difference, consider the following two code snippets entered at the REPL.

```
user=> (def integers (iterate inc 0))
#'user/integers
user=> (nth integers 1000000)
1000000
```

And:

```
user=> (nth (iterate inc 0) 1000000)
1000000
```

Although these two code snippets are identical in respect to what they do, profiling the JVM indicates that the former statement results in ~60 megabytes of heap space being utilized after the call to nth, while the latter results in no appreciable increase. Why?

In the first sample, the lazy sequence is referenced by a symbol. The sequence is initially unrealized, and takes up very little memory. However, in order to retrieve the selected value, nth must realize the sequence up to the value selected. All values from 0 to 1000000 are now cached in the sequence bound to the integers symbol, and it is this that utilizes the memory.

So why doesn't using nth in the second example use up memory as well? The answer is that nth itself does not maintain any references. As it goes through a sequence, it retrieves the rest from each entry, and drops any references to the sequence itself. The sequence created by (iterate inc 0) is supplied as an initial argument, but unlike the first example, no permanent reference to it is maintained, and nth "forgets" it almost immediately as it progresses. No cached values are ever saved, and so no memory is used.

All the built in-sequence functions, such as nth, are careful not to maintain any memory-consuming references, so ensuring proper memory usage is a responsibility of the developer. Keeping track of memory usage means, primarily, keeping track of references to lazy sequences.

It may sound complicated at first, but in time, once you're used to working with Clojure, eliminating extraneous references comes fairly easily. Clojure's own emphasis on pure functions itself greatly helps to discourage indiscriminate reference-making. The only area where it is easy to make a mistake is when writing your own sequence-consuming functions, and as long as you maintain a clear idea of which symbols reference potentially infinite sequences, it should provide no great difficulty. The important thing is to know what to look for when presented with an OutOfMemoryError.

The Sequence API

Clojure provides a complete set of sequence manipulation functions. Being familiar with them and their capabilities will save a great deal of effort, as it is often possible to eliminate a surprising amount of code with a single call to one of these functions.

Sequence Creation

The functions in this section provide various means for creating sequences, either directly or from existing data structures.

seq

The seq function takes a single argument, a collection, and returns a sequence representation of the collection. Most sequence manipulation functions automatically call seq on their arguments, so they can accept collections without requiring a manual call to seq.

```
user=> (seq [1 2 3 4 5])
(1 2 3 4 5)
```

```
user=> (seq {:a 1 :b 2 :c 3})
([:a 1] [:b 2] [:c 3])
```

vals

vals takes a single argument, a map, and returns a sequence of the values in the map.

```
user=> (vals {:key1 "value1" :key2 "value2" :key3 "value3"})
(" value1" "value2" "value3")
```

keys

keys takes a single argument, a map, and returns a sequence of the keys in the map.

```
user=> (keys {:key1 "value1" :key2 "value2" :key3 "value3"})
(:key1 :key2 :key3)
```

rseq

rseq takes a single argument, which must be a vector or a sorted map. It returns a sequence of its values in reversed order; operation returns in constant time.

```
user=> (rseq [1 2 3 4])
(4 3 2 1)
```

lazy-seq

lazy-seq is a macro which wraps a form that returns a sequence. It produces a lazy sequence, which is discussed in detail in the previous section "Constructing Lazy Sequences Directly."

repeatedly

repeatedly takes a single argument, a function with no arguments, and returns an infinite lazy sequence obtained by calling the function repeatedly. Note that if the function is a pure function, it will simply return the same value every time, since it has no arguments.

```
user=> (take 5 (repeatedly (fn []"hello")))
("hello" "hello" "hello" "hello" "hello")
```

Usually, repeatedly is more useful with an impure function, such as one based on rand-int, which returns a random integer between 0 and its argument.

```
user=> (take 5 (repeatedly (fn [] (rand-int 5))))
(3 0 4 3 2)
```

iterate

iterate takes two arguments: a function with a single argument and a value. It returns an infinite lazy sequence obtained by starting with the supplied value, and then by calling the supplied function passing the previous item in the sequence as its argument.

```
user=> (take 10 (iterate inc 5))
(5 6 7 8 9 10 11 12 13 14)
```

This example uses the increment function inc to generate an infinite sequence of integers, starting at 5. For a more detailed discussion, see the previous section, "Constructing Lazy Sequences Using Sequence Generator Functions."

repeat

repeat takes one or two arguments. The single-argument version returns an infinite lazy sequence consisting of the argument value repeated endlessly.

```
user=> (take 5 (repeat "hi"))
("hi" "hi" "hi" "hi" "hi")
```

The two-argument version takes a number as its first argument and a value as its second. It returns a lazy sequence the length of the first argument, consisting of repetitions of the second argument.

```
user=> (repeat 5 "hi")
("hi" "hi" "hi" "hi" "hi")
```

range

range takes one, two, or three arguments. The one-argument version takes a number as its argument and returns a lazy sequence of numbers from 0 to the argument (exclusive).

```
user=> (range 5)
(0 1 2 3 4)
```

The two-argument version takes two numbers as its arguments and returns a lazy sequence of numbers from the first argument (inclusive) to the second argument (exclusive).

```
user=> (range 5 10)
(5 6 7 8 9)
```

The three-argument version takes three numbers as its arguments and returns a lazy sequence of numbers from the first argument (inclusive) to the second argument (exclusive) incremented by the third argument.

```
user=> (range 4 16 2)
(4 6 8 10 12 14)
```

distinct

distinct takes a single argument, a sequence or collection. It returns a sequence obtained by removing all duplicates from the argument.

```
user=> (distinct [1 2 2 3 3 4 1])
(1 2 3 4)
```

filter

filter takes two arguments: a predicate function which takes a single argument and returns a boolean value, and a sequence/collection. Returns a lazy sequence consisting only of items in the second argument for which the predicate function returns true.

```
user=> (filter (fn [s] (= \a (first s))) ["ant" "bee" "ape" "cat" "dog"])
("ant" "ape")
```

In this example, the predicate function tests whether the first letter of its argument is an "a" character.

remove

remove is similar to filter, except that the resulting sequence contains only items for which the predicate function returns false.

```
user=> (remove (fn [s] (= \a (first s))) ["ant" "bee" "ape" "cat" "dog"])
("bee" "cat" "dog")
```

cons

cons takes two arguments, a value and a sequence/collection. It returns a sequence formed by appending the value to the sequence.

```
user=> (cons 1 [ 2 3 4])
(1 2 3 4)
```

concat

concat takes any number of arguments, all sequences/collections. It returns a lazy sequence formed by concatenating the provided sequences.

```
user=> (concat [1 2 3] '(4 5 6) [7 8 9])
(1 2 3 4 5 6 7 8 9)
```

lazy-cat

lazy-cat is a macro that takes any number of forms as arguments, all sequences/collections. It resolves to a lazy sequence formed by concatenating the provided sequences. lazy-cat differs from concat in that the expressions provided are not even evaluated until they are required. lazy-cat is, as the name suggests, like concat, but lazier. Use lazy-cat when the result might not be entirely consumed, and so the cost of even evaluating the provided forms might be avoided.

```
user=> (lazy-cat [1 2 3] '(4 5 6) [7 8 9])
(1 2 3 4 5 6 7 8 9)
```

mapcat

mapcat takes a function as its first argument and any number of sequences/collections as additional arguments. It applies the map function with the provided function to the sequence arguments, and then concatenates all the results. mapcat assumes that the supplied function returns a collection or sequence, as it applies concat to its results.

```
user=> (mapcat (fn [x] (repeat 3 x)) [1 2 3])
(1 1 1 2 2 2 3 3 3)
```

In this example, the supplied function returns a sequence of its argument repeated 3 times. mapcat concatenates the result of applying the function to each of the supplied sequences/collections.

cycle

cycle takes a single argument, a sequence/collection. It returns a lazy infinite sequence obtained by successively repeating the values in the supplied sequence/collection.

```
user=> (take 10 (cycle [:a :b :c]))
(:a :b :c :a :b :c :a)
```

interleave

interleave takes any number of sequences/collections as arguments. It returns a lazy sequence obtained by taking the first value from each argument sequence, then the second, then the third, etc. It stops when one of the argument sequences runs out of values.

```
user=> (interleave [:a :b :c] [1 2 3])
(:a 1 :b 2 :c 3)
```

```
user=> (interleave [:a :b :c] (iterate inc 1)]
(:a 1 :b 2 :c 3)
```

```
user=> (interleave [:a :b :c] [1 2 3] [\A \B \C])
(:a 1 \A :b 2 \B :c 3 \C)
```

interpose

interpose takes two arguments, a value and a sequence/collection. It returns a lazy sequence obtained by inserting the supplied value between the values in the sequence.

```
user=> (interpose :a [1 2 3 4])
(1 :a 2 :a 3 :a 4 :a 5)
```

rest

rest takes a single sequence/collection as an argument. It returns a sequence of all items in the passed sequence except the first. If there are no more items, it returns an empty sequence.

```
user=> (rest [1 2 3 4])
(2 3 4)
```

```
user=> (rest [])
()
```

next

next takes a single sequence/collection as an argument. It returns a sequence of all items in the passed sequence, except the first. If there are no more items, it returns nil.

```
user=> (next [1 2 3 4])
(2 3 4)

user=> (next [])
nil
```

drop

drop takes two arguments, a number and a sequence/collection. It returns a sequence of all items after the provided number of items. If there are no more items, drop returns an empty sequence.

```
user=> (drop 2 [:a :b :c :d :e])
(:c :d :e)
```

drop-while

drop-while takes two arguments, a predicate function taking a single argument and a sequence/collection. It returns a sequence of all items in the original sequence, starting from the first item for which the predicate function returns false.

```
user=> (drop-while pos? [2 1 5 -3 6 -2 -1])
(-3 6 -2 -1)
```

This example uses the pos? function as a predicate. pos? returns true for all numbers greater than zero, otherwise false.

take

take takes two arguments, a number and a sequence/collection. It returns a sequence consisting of the first items in the provided sequence. The returned sequence will be limited in length to the provided number.

```
user=> (take 2 [1 2 3 4 5])
(1 2)
```

take-nth

take-nth takes two arguments, a number and a sequence/collection. It returns a sequence of items from the supplied sequence, taking the first item and every Nth item, where N is the supplied number.

```
user=> (take-nth 3 [1 2 3 4 5 6 7 8 9 10])
(1 4 7 10)
```

take-while

take-while takes two arguments, a predicate function taking a single argument and a sequence/collection. It returns a sequence of all items in the original sequence, up until the first item for which the predicate function returns false.

```
user=> (take-while pos? [2 1 5 -3 6 -2 -1])
(2 1 5)
```

drop-last

drop-last takes one or two arguments. The one argument version takes a sequence/collection. It returns a sequence containing all but the last item in the provided sequence

```
user=> (drop-last [1 2 3 4 5])
(1 2 3 4)
```

The two-argument version takes a number and a sequence/collection. It returns a sequence containing all but the last N items in the provided sequence, where N is the provided number.

```
user=> (drop-last  2 [1 2 3 4 5])
(1 2 3)
```

reverse

reverse takes a single argument, a sequence/collection. It returns a sequence of the items in reverse order. reverse is not lazy.

```
user=> (reverse [1 2 3 4 5])
(5 4 3 2 1)
```

sort

sort takes one or two arguments. The one-argument version takes a sequence/collection and returns a sequence of the items sorted according to their natural ordering.

```
user=> (sort [2 3 5 4 1])
(1 2 3 4 5)
```

The two-argument version takes an object implementing java.util.Comparator and a sequence collection. It returns a sequence of items sorted according to the comparator.

sort-by

sort-by takes two or three arguments. The two-argument version takes a key function which takes a single argument, and a sequence/collection. It returns a sequence of the items sorted by the values returned by applying they key function to the item. The key function should then return a naturally sortable value, such as a string or a number.

```
user=> (sort-by (fn [n] (/ 1 n)) [2 3 5 4 1])
(5 4 3 2 1)
```

This example supplies a function that returns the reciprocal of its argument as a key function. The result sequence is ordered not by the values themselves, but by the result of applying the key function to them. That is, they are ordered by their reciprocals.

The two-argument version takes a key function, an object implementing java.util.Comparator and a sequence collection. It functions the same as the two argument version, except it uses the supplied comparator to sort the results of the key function.

split-at

split-at takes two arguments: a number and a sequence/collection. It returns a vector of two items. The first item in the result vector is a sequence obtained by taking the first N items from the supplied sequence, where N is the supplied number. The second item in the result vector is the rest of the items in the supplied sequence.

```
user=> (split-at 2 [:a :b :c :d :e :f])
[(:a :b) (:c :d :e :f)]
```

split-with

split-with takes two arguments: a predicate function taking a single argument and a sequence/collection. It returns a vector of two items. The first item in the result vector is a sequence obtained by taking items from the supplied sequence until the first item where applying the supplied predicate returns false. The second item in the result vector contains the rest of the items in the supplied sequence.

```
user=> (split-with pos? [2 1 5 -3 6 -2 -1])
[(2 1 5) (-3 6 -2 -1)]
```

partition

partition takes two or three arguments. The two argument version takes a number and a sequence/collection and returns a lazy sequence of lazy sequences. Each child sequence is N items long and populated by every N items from the provided sequence, where N is the provided number.

```
user=> (partition 2 [:a :b :c :d :e :f])
((:a :b) (:c :d) (:e :f))
```

The three-argument version takes two numbers, and a sequence/collection. It works the same way as the two argument version, with the exception that the child sequences are populated at offsets given by the second number provided. This allows overlap of items between the child sequences.

```
user=> (partition 2 1 [:a :b :c :d :e :f])
((:a :b) (:b :c) (:c :d) (:d :e) (:e :f))
```

map

map takes a function as its first argument and any number of collections/sequences as additional arguments. The provided function should take the same number of arguments as there are additional sequences. It returns a lazy sequence obtained by applying the provided function to each item in the provided sequence(s).

```
user=> (map pos? [2 1 5 -3 6 -2 -1])
(true true true false true false false)
```

```
user=> (map + [2 4 8] [1 3 5])
(3 7 13)
```

first

first takes a single sequence/collection as an argument. It returns the first item in the sequence, or nil if the sequence is empty.

```
user=> (first [1 2 3 4])
1
```

second

second takes a single sequence/collection as an argument. It returns the second item in the sequence, or nil if the sequence is empty.

```
user=> (second [1 2 3 4])
2
```

nth

nth takes two arguments: a sequence/collection and a number. It returns the Nth item of the provided sequence, where N is the provided number. Sequences are indexed from zero, so (nth sequence 0) is equivalent to (first sequence). It throws an error if the sequence has fewer than N items.

```
user=> (nth [:a :b :c :d] 2)
:c
```

last

last takes a single sequence/collection as an argument. It returns the last item in the sequence. If the sequence is empty, returns nil.

```
user=> (last [1 2 3 4])
4
```

reduce

reduce takes two or three arguments. In the two argument version, the first argument is a function which must take two arguments and the second argument is a sequence/collection. reduce applies the supplied function to the first two items in the supplied sequence, then calls the supplied function again with the result of the first call and the next item, and so on for each item in the sequence.

```
user=> (reduce + [1 2 3 4 5])
15
```

In this example, reduce applies the addition function to a list of integers, resulting in their sum total.

The three argument version is similar, except that it takes a function, an initial value, and a sequence/collection. The function is applied to the initial value and the first item of the sequence, instead of the first two items of the collection. The following example illustrates this by building a map from a sequence, using each item as a key and its reciprocal as a value. An empty map is provided as the initial value:

```
user=> (reduce (fn [my-map value]
                       (assoc my-map value (/ 1 value)))
               {}
               [1 2 3 4 5])
{5 1/5, 4 1/4, 3 1/3, 2 1/2, 1 1}
```

apply

apply takes two or more arguments. The first argument is a function and the last argument is a sequence/collection. Other arguments may be any values. It returns the result of calling the supplied function with the supplied values, and the values of the supplied sequence, as arguments. Calling (apply f a b [c d e]) is identical to calling (f a b c d e). The advantage of apply is that it is possible to build dynamic sequences of arguments.

```
user=> (apply + 1 [2 3])
6
```

An example using apply on a dynamic list of arguments: calling + with the integers 0–5 as arguments. This call is equivalent to (+ 1 2 3 4 5), except the argument list is generated dynamically.

```
user=> (apply + (range 1 6))
15
```

empty?

empty? takes a single sequence/collection as an argument. It returns true if the sequence has no items, otherwise false.

```
user=> (empty? [1 2 3 4])
false
```

```
user=> (empty? [])
true
```

some

some takes two arguments: a predicate function taking a single argument and a sequence/collection. It returns the value of the predicate function if there is at least one item in the provided sequence for which it does not return false or nil, else nil.

```
user=> (some (fn [n] (< n 5)) [6 9 7 3])
true
```

```
user=> (some (fn [n] (< n 5)) [6 9 7 5])
nil
```

every?

every? takes two arguments: a predicate function taking a single argument and a sequence/collection. It returns true if the predicate function is true for every value in the sequence, otherwise false.

```
user=> (every? (fn [n] (< n 5)) [2 1 4 3])
true
```

```
user=> (every? (fn [n] (< n 5)) [2 1 5 3])
false
```

dorun

dorun takes one or two arguments: a lazy sequence or optionally a number and a lazy sequence. It causes the lazy sequence to be realized, solely for side effects. dorun always returns nil and does not retain the head of the list, so it will not consume memory.

To demonstrate, the following example applies the map function to a lazy sequence, supplying the println function to map. Normally, println is not a good candidate for an argument to map, since it executes only for side effects and always returns nil.

```
user=> (def result (map println (range 1 5)))
#'user/result
user=> (dorun result)
1
2
3
4
nil
```

In this example, the result symbol is bound to a lazy sequence, the product of map. The actual *values* of this sequence are all nil, since they are the result of calling println. They are unused in this example. However, whenever the generator function (println) for the sequence is called, it results in a side effect. Since the sequence returned by map is lazy, the generator function is not called until the call to dorun, which forces the sequence to be sequentially evaluated.

If a numeric parameter is provided, dorun evaluates the sequence only as far as that index.

```
user=> (def result (map println (range 1 10)))
#'user/result
user=> (dorun 2 result)
1
2
```

```
3
nil
```

Be very careful to always use a numeric parameter to dorun when calling it with an infinite sequence or else the execution will never terminate.

doall

doall, rdentical to dorun, with the exception that as the sequence is evaluated, it is saved and returned by the function. In essence, doall returns a non-lazy version of a lazy sequence. As such, it will result in memory consumption proportional to the size of the sequence. Invoking on an infinite sequence without a numeric parameter will result in an OutOfMemoryError as the system attempts to cache a sequence of infinite length.

```
user=> (def result (map println (range 1 5)))
#'user/result
user=> (doall result)
1
2
3
4
(nil nil nil nil)
```

Note how the function, after executing the generator function for side effects, also returns the actual sequence of values resulting from the call to map. In this case, they are all nil, the return value of println.

Summary

The more you use sequences, the more you will come to appreciate them. Having a highly integrated, extremely powerful generic collection management library at your fingertips is hard to do without when you go back to a language without it.

When writing idiomatic Clojure, one cannot use sequences too much. Any point in code where there is more than one object is a candidate for using a sequence to manage the collection. Doing so provides for free all the sequence functions, both built-in and user generated. They will greatly aid in writing expressive, succinct programs.

■ ■ ■

CHAPTER 6

State Management

State in an Immutable World

As much as possible, Clojure advocates eliminating state from programs. In general, data should be passed and returned from functions in a purely functional way. It keeps things clean, protected, and parallelizable.

Often, however, that's simply not possible. The real world is full of changing concepts and so real programs are full of state. If you're writing a word processor, the current document has a state. If you're writing a game, the objects in the game world exist have state. If you're writing financial software, the amount of money in an account is state. This is a fact of the way the world is and the way humans think, and programs need to be able to model it effectively.

With today's concurrent environments, effective modeling of state is not just something nice to have, but absolutely necessary to get anything done. Even aside from the concurrency issues, however, there are many benefits of languages which have a clear conceptualization of state. Even in a single threaded program, explicit managed state is preferable to having state smeared across the entire application, and Clojure provides just that: efficient explicitly managed state.

The Old Way

Most programming languages model state via a fairly naive process. There are *things*, represented by variables or objects, and these things can change. But how and when they change is not well defined. Usually, programs "bash objects in place"—each line of code is free to reach in and push arbitrary changes to any part of any *thing* as it executes. The only way to preserve consistency and prevent bugs caused by two changes happening at once is to place safeguards around each and every *thing*, ensuring that only one process can interact with a given *thing* at once. These are known as locks.

The problem with locks is that they're hard to get right. In order to make them correct, the first reaction is to use more of them, which only causes another problem: extensive use of locks solves the problems introduced by concurrency by, effectively, reducing the level of concurrency that is actually possible. It doesn't matter how many threads a program has running, if they all must queue up to access an object one at a time, then at that point they might as well be running in a single thread.

However, with the view that there are only mutable, changeable *things*, and without having well-defined semantics for how they change, locks are the only option. For a more effective approach to state, it is necessary to reevaluate and find better definitions for what *things* are, and establish clear rules for how they change.

State and Identity

Clojure introduces a philosophical and conceptual paradigm shift in its treatment of *things*. It takes the standard notion of a *thing* (an object or a variable) and decomposes it into two separate concepts—*state* and *identity*.[1] Every *thing* has both a state and an identity. State is a value associated with an identity at a particular moment in time, whereas identity is the part of a thing that does *not* change, and creates the link between many different states at many different times. The value of each state is immutable and cannot change. Rather, change is modeled by the identity being updated to refer to a *different* state entirely.

For example, when I was a child, in 1990, I was a very, very different person than I am now in 2010, and it is very probable that I will be a different person still when I am much older in 2050. $Luke_{1990}$, $Luke_{2010}$ and $Luke_{2050}$ are quite different people—you could go as far as to say that they don't have that many similarities at all. And yet, they do have a relationship, a constant identity—they are all me, Luke VanderHart.

In Clojure's logical terminology, $Luke_{1990}$, $Luke_{2010}$ and $Luke_{2050}$ are all distinct values—distinct states. My name, Luke VanderHart, is the identity that links them all together. Like Clojure's values, these states are immutable. I may be able to change future versions of myself, but $Luke_{1990}$ is set in stone. I can no longer do anything to change who that person was or is. Currently, the identity Luke VanderHart has $Luke_{2010}$ as its state. Next year, it will have a new state: $Luke_{2011}$, which will likely be very similar to $Luke_{2010}$ but with subtle differences. Actually, in Clojure's model, every time I change at all, it generates a new state: millisecond by millisecond, I have new values associated with my identity as I have different thoughts, feelings, and motions. I am a near infinity of distinct, unchangeable persons, all slightly different, all linked by a common identity.

Another example is my bank account, a much less philosophical example and one more likely to be modeled in an actual program. As I spend money and receive paychecks, the balance of my bank account fluctuates. Clearly, it is something that needs to be modeled as changeable state. In this case, the identity which remains constant throughout the program is "my account"—call the identity `account-balance`. The state, then, is the amount of money in the account at a given time. For example, it might start at $1000. If I deposit a check for $100, then the `account-balance` identity is updated to point to a new state, $1100. Note that I have not *changed* the value of the state—changing the integer 1000 to 1100 is a clear impossibility: 1000 and 1100 are distinct mathematical values. The state has not changed, rather, the identity of `account-balance` now points to a *new* state. The update takes place atomically; there is no intermediate state where the value of `account-balance` is half-set. At any point in the program, it is safe to query the current state of `account-balance`.

State and Identity in Clojure

In Clojure code, states are simply any of Clojure's data types. They can be primitives, such as numbers or strings, or more complex structures built out of lists, maps, and sets. The only limitation on values that can be used as states is that they ought to be immutable. If you use a mutable structure (such as a Java object) as a state, you haven't actually accomplished anything: Clojure's state management system is founded on the premise that values themselves are immutable, and it can provide no guarantees of consistency or isolation for mutable objects.

Identities are modeled using one of the three *reference types*: refs, agents, atoms and vars. Each implements the conceptual model outlined previously; each represents an identity and points to a state.

---

[1] For the definitive discussion of state and identity, see Rich Hickey's essay "On State and Identity" at `http://clojure.org/state`.

They differ in the semantics of how they can be updated to refer to new state values and are useful in different situations. Between them, they can handle just about any state management task:

- Use refs to manage *synchronous, coordinated* state

- Use agents to manage *asynchronous, independent* state

- Use atoms to manage *synchronous, independent* state

Coordinated vs. Independent State

One requirement common to many systems is that updates to certain identities be coordinated to ensure data integrity. Coordinated updates can't just take one identity into account—they have to manage the states of several interdependent identities to ensure that they are all updated at the same time and that none are left out. The most common example of coordinated state is a transfer of funds between two bank accounts: money deposited into one account must also be subtracted from the other, and these two actions must occur as a single, coordinated event, or not at all. Clojure uses refs to provide coordinated state.

The alternative to coordinated state is independent state. Independent identities stand on their own and can have their state updated without concern for other identities. This still needs to be controlled in some way, but internally, this is usually a more efficient process than coordinating changes to multiple identities. Therefore, updates to independent identities are usually faster than updates to coordinated identities; use them in preference to refs unless coordinated access is required. Clojure provides agents and atoms as independent identity reference types.

Synchronous vs. Asynchronous Updates

Synchronous updates to the values identities occur immediately, in the same thread from which they are invoked. The execution of the code does not continue until the update has taken place, as most programmers would expect. This is the default way instructions execute in most programming languages. Updates to the values of refs and atoms are both handled synchronously in Clojure.

Asynchronous updates do *not* occur immediately, but at some unspecified point in the (near) future, usually in another thread. The code execution continues immediately from the point at which the update was invoked, without waiting for it to complete. Extensive use of asynchronous updates is useful for introducing concurrency into programs, and for more flexible event-based programming models. However, there is no guarantee when the effect of an asynchronous update will actually be in place. It will nearly always be instantaneous from a human scale, but from a code perspective, it might not be. For example, if one line of code updates an asynchronous identity, and the very next line of code in the same thread reads its state, it will probably get the old state. Don't use asynchronous identities where your code depends on the update happening right away. Agents are Clojure's implementation of asynchronously updated identities.

Refs and Transactions

Refs are Clojure's implementation of synchronous, coordinated identities. Each is a distinct identity, but operations on them can be run inside a *transaction*, guaranteeing that multiple identities whose values depend on each other are always in a consistent state. Refs provide access to Clojure's state-of-the-art Software Transactional Memory (STM) system.

Creating and Accessing refs

To create a ref, use the built-in ref function, which takes a single argument: the initial value of the ref:

```
user=> (def my-ref (ref 5))
#'user/my-ref
```

This code does two things: creates a ref with an initial state of the integer 5 and binds the ref to a var, my-ref. It is an important distinction: the var is *not* the ref itself, it is just *bound* to the ref. If you try to get the value of the var, you get the following:

```
user=> my-ref
#<Ref@1010058: 5>
```

my-ref is a var like any other. It just has a ref as its bound value, which is seen here. "#<Ref@1010058: 5>" is the string debugging representation of a ref. To actually get the current state of the ref, it is necessary to use the dereference function deref:

```
user=> (deref my-ref)
5
```

The deref function always takes a single argument, which must resolve to a ref and returns the current state of the ref. Because the deref function is used so frequently, there is a shorthand for it: the @ symbol. Prefixing an expression with @ is identical to calling deref on it:

```
user=> (deref my-ref)
5
user=> @my-ref
5
```

The shorthand form makes it easier to dereference symbols within expressions:

```
user=> (+ 1 @my-ref)
6
```

Dereferencing a ref always returns its state, immediately. Refs are never locked (at least, not in a traditional sense) and deref does not block while waiting for a transaction to complete. It always just returns a snapshot of the ref's current state. This means that if you call deref twice, outside of a transaction, it is possible that you will get two different values.

Updating refs

There are several different functions which can be used to update the values of refs. They differ in their performance implications, and are explained in detail in the following sections, but they have one thing in common: they are designed exclusively for use within transactions. Executing any of them outside a transaction always throws an error.

Transactions

For anyone who has worked with relational databases, Clojure's transactions will be a familiar concept: they operate in almost exactly the same way as their database counterparts. Essentially, all updates contained within a single transaction are committed to the application state *atomically*, at the same time. Either all the updates occur at the same time, or none do. Consistency across ref values is guaranteed.

Transactions are also *isolated,* which means that no transaction can see the effects of any other transaction while it is running. When a transaction begins, it takes a snapshot of all the ref values involved. Subsequent updates to those values from outside the transaction are invisible to code within the transaction, just as changes made within the transaction are invisible to the outside world until it is finished and committed. Of course, changes made within a transaction *are* visible within the same transaction. Dereferencing a ref within a transaction always returns the "in-transaction" value of the ref, which reflects any updates that have been made since the beginning of the transaction.

Additionally, transactions nest. If a transaction is initiated while already inside a transaction, the inner transaction simply becomes part of the outer transaction and will not commit until the outer transaction commits.

Transactions are conceptually lock-free and optimistic. This means that transactions don't wait for other transactions to complete before they begin. Transactions will never block a thread while waiting for another update. However, it doesn't remove the possibility that multiple transactions updating the same ref can conflict. A transaction might complete, only to find that the refs it is trying to update are stale and have already been updated by another transaction. In this case, the transaction simply retries, taking a snapshot of the new values and running itself again. The system prioritizes commits, insuring that no matter how much contention there is for a particular ref, each transaction is guaranteed to complete eventually.

High-concurrency, high-contention scenarios *will* result in a slowdown of the STM system as many transactions are retried. However, in most cases it will still end up faster than the equivalent system using locks. Even in the worst case, where a perfectly designed system of locks is provably faster than STM, Clojure argues that STM is still worthwhile due to the decreased cognitive load and simplicity of the solutions.

Many consider the benefits of STM to be roughly analogous to managed memory and garbage collection: most the time they are more than fast enough, and they save so much effort from programmers and software architects that the occasional scenario where they underperform the meticulously, complicated manual solution can be accepted.

Tools for Updating refs

The most important form when working with refs is the `dosync` macro. `dosync` initiates a transaction and takes any number of additional forms. Each provided form is evaluated sequentially within a transaction. The value of the final form is returned after committing the transaction. If an exception is thrown from any of the provided forms, the transaction is terminated without committing.

For actually updating the state of a ref, the most basic function is `ref-set`. `ref-set` takes two arguments: a ref and a value. It sets the state of the reference to be the value, and then returns the value. Of course, it must be run within a transaction established by `dosync`.

For example, the following code:

```
user=> (def my-ref (ref 5))
#'user/my-ref
user=> @my-ref
5
```

```
user=> (dosync (ref-set my-ref 6))
6
user=> @my-ref
6
```

To emphasize, ref-set and all other ref functions may *only* be called from within a transaction. Trying to call ref-set outside of a transaction throws the following error:

user=> (ref-set my-ref 7)
java.lang.IllegalStateException: No transaction running

Another common function for updating refs is alter. alter takes a ref, a function, and any number of additional arguments. It calls the provided function with the in-transaction value of the ref as its first argument and the other provided arguments as additional arguments. It sets the value of the ref to the return value of the function and returns the same value.

user=> (def my-ref (ref 5))
#'user/my-ref
user=> @my-ref
5
user=> (dosync (alter my-ref + 3))
8
user=> @my-ref
8

▨ **Note** The function provided to alter *must* be free of side effects and return a purely functional transformation of the ref value. This is because the function may be executed multiple times as the STM retries the transaction. If the function has side effects, including updates to other identities, they will be executed at least once, but potentially an arbitrary number of times if the update is highly contentious., Almost always, this will have unexpected and undesired results. Double check that all functions passed to alter are pure.

Some might wonder why both ref-set and alter are provided, given that they're essentially just different ways of doing the same thing—setting the state of a ref. The distinction is not so much in their actual functionality as in what they imply to someone reading the code. alter usually indicates that the new value of the ref is a function of the old, that it is an update that is related to it in some way. ref-set implies that the old value is being obliterated and replaced with the new. Under the hood, there isn't any difference, but when trying to understand a program, it can be a great help to see at a glance whether the value being set is tied to the old value or not.

The final function used to update refs is commute. commute has the same signature and basic functionality of alter, but with one important difference: in a contended transaction, rather than restarting the whole transaction as it normally would, it goes ahead and uses the new value instead of the in-transaction value when performing its calculation. This means that commute operations are less contentious, and will achieve much better performance in high-contention scenarios.

It also means that commute operations are *not* perfectly isolated within a transaction. However, if the function passed to commute is logically or mathematically *commutative*, it makes no difference.

Commutative functions are those which may be applied in any order without impacting the end result. In contentious transactions which use commute, that is exactly what happens. commute buys efficiency by making the assumption that it can apply the update in any order relative to other updates. Therefore, you should only use commute if the provided function can be applied in any order without affecting the outcome (or if you don't care whether it does). If you use commute with a function that isn't guaranteed to be logically commutative, you will likely see inconsistent, unpredictable behavior.

An example of using commute appropriately (since + is a naturally commutative operation):

```
user=> (def my-ref (ref 5))
#'user/my-ref
user=> @my-ref
5
user=> (dosync (commute my-ref + 3))
8
user=> @my-ref
8
```

There is one more function that operates on refs: ensure. It takes a single argument, a ref. Like the other ref functions, it can only be used inside a transaction. Unlike other ref functions, it doesn't actually change the state of a ref. What it *does* do is to force a transaction retry if the ensured ref changes during the transaction, just as it would if it were a ref you updated. Of course, you wouldn't see such changes inside the transaction in any case, due to transaction isolation. But normally, if you don't update a ref in a transaction, that ref is not included in the consistency guarantees of the final commit. If you want to ensure that a ref you don't update is nevertheless unchanged after a transaction for coordination reasons, use ensure on it within the transaction.

Examples

Listing 6-1 illustrates the classic example of transactional behavior previously mentioned, transferring money from one bank account to another. This is a scenario in which coordination between the two pieces of state—the two accounts—is vitally important. If the values were not coordinated, it would be possible, however briefly, to be in a state in which the money was added to one account but not yet subtracted from the other (or vice versa). Using refs and transactions ensures that the account addition and subtraction occur atomically.

Listing 6-1. Bank Accounts in STM

```
(def account1 (ref 1000))
(def account2 (ref 1500))

(defn transfer
    "transfers amount of money from a to b"
    [a b amount]
    (dosync
        (alter a - amount)
        (alter b + amount)))

(transfer account1 account2 300)
(transfer account2 account1 50)
```

```
(println "Account #1:" @account1)
(println "Account #2:" @account2)
```

Running this code yields the expected output after the two transactions. Because the transaction is guaranteed by Clojure's STM, the results would be the consistent no matter how many threads were concurrently updating the accounts. In this case, the output is:

Account #1: 750
Account #2: 1750

The following example is much more complex, and demonstrates how refs can be stored in any data structure (not just def'd at the top level), how they can have any data structure as their value, not just integers, and how even refs can be part of the value of another ref. It is just a basic example of using refs: you will probably want to approach the ref structure in an actual program with a great deal more thought. In general, it's better to be judicious and use as few refs as will meet your needs.

The program represents a rudimentary address book. The main data structure is a vector of contacts. It is contained in a ref, since you need to be able to update it and it starts out empty. Each contact is a map containing first name and last name. Rather than storing the entries directly, though, they are each stored as a ref themselves, since each is an individually updateable piece of state (see Listing 6-2).

Lilsting 6-2. An Address Book in STM

```
(def my-contacts (ref []))

(defn add-contact
    "adds a contact to the provided contact list"
    [contacts contact]
    (dosync
        (alter contacts conj (ref contact))))

(defn print-contacts
    "prints a list of contacts"
    [contacts]
    (doseq [c @contacts]
                    (println (str "Name: " (@c :lname) ", " (@c :fname)))
                ))


(add-contact my-contacts {:fname "Luke" :lname "VanderHart"})
(add-contact my-contacts {:fname "Stuart" :lname "Sierra"})
(add-contact my-contacts {:fname "John" :lname "Doe"})

(print-contacts my-contacts)
```

Running the scripts creates a list of contacts, adds several contacts to it (as refs), and then prints the list, yielding:

Name: VanderHart , Luke
Name: Sierra, Stuart
Name: Doe, John

Note how the print-contacts function needs to dereference the contacts list and also each contact before it can use it, since both are references.

Now, as an example of coordinated access to multiple refs, consider the task of adding an "initials" field to each contact, but doing it in a coordinated way so there is no chance that any contact might be left out. This is slightly contrived, but is similar to many real-world tasks: the goal is to make it impossible for there to be a state in which some contacts have initials and not others. This can be done with Listing 6-3's code added after the previous code. It is split into multiple functions for greater clarity.

Listing 6-3. Adding Initials to the Address Book

```
(defn add-initials
    "adds initials to a single contact and returns it"
    [contact]
    (assoc contact :initials
        (str (first (contact :fname)) (first (contact :lname)))))

(defn add-all-initials
    "adds initials to each of the contacts in a list of contacts"
    [contacts]
    (dosync
        (doseq [contact (ensure contacts)]
          (alter contact add-initials))))
(defn print-contacts-and-initials
    "prints a list of contacts, with initials"
    [contacts]
    (dorun (map (fn [c]
                          (println (str "Name: " (@c :lname) ", " (@c :fname) " (" (@c
:initials) ")")))
                    @contacts)))

(defn print-contacts-and-initials
    "prints a list of contacts, with initials"
    [contacts]
    (doseq [c @contacts]
      (println (str "Name: " (@c :lname) ", " (@c :fname) " (" (@c :initials) ")"))))


(add-all-initials my-contacts)
(print-contacts-and-initials my-contacts)
```

When executed the code prints off the same names as before, with their initials added:

```
Name: VanderHart , Luke (LV)
Name: Sierra, Stuart (SS)
Name: Doe, John (JD)
```

The key function which actually deals with the refs is add-all-initials. It first opens a transaction, and then calls ensure on the contacts ref. This is to make sure that if contacts is updated while the transaction is running, it will be restarted. I want to include *all* of the contacts, and without the ensure, if contacts were updated with a new contact after the transaction had begun it would not be included.

Then, for each contact (using doseq), it alters it using the add-initials function, setting it to a map containing an initials key. Because all the alter statements are run in the same transaction, the update to all the contacts is atomic: from outside the transaction, all the contacts are updated to a value with the new field instantaneously.

Because the whole operation never blocks, other threads involved in reading the contacts list continue to do so at full speed. If another transaction in another thread tries to write to a contact at the same time, one transaction or the other might have to retry, but in the end, it's still guaranteed that everything that needs to happen will eventually happen to each contact, and that they will remain in a coordinated state.

Atoms

Atoms are Clojure's implementation of synchronous, uncoordinated identities. When updated the change is applied before proceeding with the current thread and the update occurs atomically. All future dereferences to the atom from all threads will resolve to the new value.

Atoms are based on the atomic classes in the Java java.util.concurrent.atomic package. They provide a way to update values atomically with no chance of race conditions corrupting the update. Unlike the Java atomic package, however, they are lock-free. Therefore, reads of atoms are guaranteed never to block and updates will retry if the atom's value is updated while they are in progress, just like refs.

In practice, atoms are used almost exactly like refs, except that since they are uncoordinated they do not need to participate in transactions.

Using Atoms

To create an atom, use the atom function, which takes a single argument and returns an atom with the argument as its initial state. To retrieve the value of an atom, use the deref function (the same one used for refs) or the @ shorthand.

```
user=> (def my-atom (atom 5))
#'user/my-atom
user=> @my-atom
5
```

As with refs, there are two ways to update the value of an atom: swap! and reset!. The swap! function takes an atom, a function, and any number of additional arguments. It updates (swaps) the value of the atom for the value obtained by calling the supplied function with the current value of the atom as the first argument, and the other provided arguments as additional arguments. It returns the new value of the atom. Like the function provided to alter the function passed to swap! may be executed multiple times and should therefore be free of side effects.

The following example uses the atom set up in the previous snippet and passes the addition function, along with an additional argument of 3.

```
user=> (swap! my-atom + 3)
8
user=> @my-atom
8
```

The reset! function sets the value of an atom regardless of the current value. It takes two arguments (the atom and a value) and returns the new value of the atom.

```
user=> (reset! my-atom  1)
1
user=> @my-atom
1
```

When to Use Atoms

In practice, atoms aren't used as frequently as refs in programs. Since they can't coordinate with other pieces of state, their usefulness is limited to scenarios in which an identity is truly, logically independent from other identities in the system.

For cases where an identity *is* independent, however, atoms are the right choice. They avoid much of the overhead associated with refs and are very fast, particularly to read. They don't have the parallelism implications of agents (discussed in the next section), and overall are the most lightweight of Clojure's identity types.

One example of a case where atoms are very useful is for caching values. Cached values need to be accessible quickly, but aren't dependent on the rest of the system's state. Clojure's memoize function (which caches the results of calling a function and is described more fully in Chapter 14 uses atoms internally to maintain its cache.

Asynchronous Agents

Agents are one of Clojure's more unique and powerful features. Like refs and atoms, they are identities and adhere to Clojure's philosophy of identity and state. Unlike refs and atoms, however, updates to their values occur asynchronously in a separate system managed thread pool dedicated to managing agent state.

This implies that agents are not only a means of storing and managing state in a concurrent environment (although they certainly are that), but are also a tool for *introducing* concurrency into a program. Using agents, there is no need to manually spawn threads, manage thread pools, or explicitly cause any other kind of concurrency. Agents are identity types, and just as easy to use and update as refs or atoms, but have concurrency thrown in "for free."

Creating and Updating Agents

Agents can be created by using the agent function, which takes a single value as the initial value of the agent. Like other Clojure identities, the value ought to be immutable.

```
user=> (def my-agent (agent 5))
#'user/my-agent
```

Also, like the other Clojure identities, the current value of an agent can always be obtained immediately without blocking by dereferencing it using the deref (or @) function.

```
user=> @my-agent
5
```

The value of an agent can be updated by dispatching an action function using the send or send-off function. The call to send returns immediately in the current thread (returning the agent itself). At some undetermined point in the future, in another thread, the action function provided to send will be applied to the agent and its return value will be used as new the value of the agent.

send takes any number of arguments. The first two are the agent and the action function, the rest are additional arguments to be passed to the update function whenever it executes. For example, to send an update to the agent previously defined:

```
user=> (send my-agent + 3)
#'user/my-agent
```

Then, at some point in the future, the new value of the agent can be retrieved:

```
user=> @my-agent
8
```

There is no hard guarantee about when the update action will be applied, although usually it is nearly immediate from a human perspective. Don't write code that depends on an agent's value being updated at any given time: agents are asynchronous and can't provide guarantees about exactly when their actions will occur.

send-off has an identical signature and behavior as send. The only difference is that the two functions hint at different performance implications to the underlying agent runtime. Use send for actions that are mostly CPU-intensive, and send-off for actions that are expected to spend time blocking on IO. This allows the agent runtime to optimize appropriately. If you use the "wrong" method, everything will still work, but the overall throughput of the agent system will be lower, since it will be optimizing for the wrong type of action.

Update Semantics

Although agents provide no guarantee as to *when* an action will take effect, update dispatches *do* follow certain rules that can be relied upon:

- Actions to any individual agent are applied serially, not concurrently. Multiple updates to the same agent won't overwrite each other or encounter race conditions.

- Multiple actions sent to an agent from the same thread will be applied in the order in which they were sent. Obviously, no such guarantees can be made about actions sent from different threads.

- If an action function contains additional dispatches to agents, either to itself or other agents, dispatches are saved and are not actually called until after the action function returns and the agent's value has been updated. This allows actions on an agent to trigger further actions without having the updates conflict.

- If an update is dispatched to an agent within a STM transaction (for example, a dosync expression), the dispatch is not sent until the transaction is committed. This means that it is safe to dispatch updates to atoms from within STM transactions.

Errors and Agents

Because action functions dispatched to agents occur asynchronously in a separate thread, they need a special error-handling mechanism. Normally, exceptions are thrown from the location in the thread in which they occur, but if an action function throws an exception, there's no way of determining that it occurred, except for the built-in agent error handling.

Agents have one of two possible failure modes :fail or :continue. If an exception is thrown while processing an action, and the agent's failure mode is :continue, the agent continues as if the action which caused the error had never happened, after calling an optional error-handler function. If, on the other hand, its failure mode is :fail, the agent is put into a failed state, and will not accept any more actions until it is restarted (although it saves its current action queue).

By default, agents with an error handler defined have a failure mode of :continue. If they don't, then the default is :fail. The failure mode of an agent can also be set explicitly using the set-error-mode! function, which takes two arguments: an agent and a mode keyword. For example, the following code:

```
user=> (set-error-mode! my-agent :continue)
nil
```

You can check the current failure mode of an agent using the error-mode function:

```
user=> (error-mode my-agent)
:continue
```

Agents can be assigned an error handler using the set-error-handler! function, which takes an agent and an error function as arguments. The error function will be called whenever an action causes an exception to be thrown or sets the agent to an invalid value. It must itself take two arguments: an agent and the exception. For example, the code that follows:

```
user=> (set-error-handler! my-agent (fn [agt ex] ( … ))
nil
```

Typically, the error handler is used to log an error, or implement some correction to ensure that it doesn't happen again. You can also retrieve the current error handler for an agent using the error-handler function, which takes a single agent as an argument and returns its error handler function.

Dealing with Agents in a Failed State

Agents currently in a failure state throw an exception on any attempt to call send or send-off on them (although dereferencing will still return the last good value of the agent). For example, dividing by zero throws the agent into a failed state in the following example:

```
user=> (def an-agent (agent 10))
#'user/an-agent
user=> (send an-agent / 0)
#<Agent@1afa486: 10>
user=> (send an-agent + 1)
java.lang.RuntimeException: Agent is failed, needs restart
```

To inspect the current errors on an agent, use the agent-error function and pass it the agent as a single argument:

```
user=> (agent-error an-agent)
#<ArithmeticException java.langArithmeticException: Divide by zero>
```

In order to put the agent back into a working state, you must call the `restart-agent` function. `restart-agent` takes as its arguments an agent, a new state, and any number of additional keyword option/value pairs. The only currently implemented option is `:clear-actions` with a boolean value.

When `restart-agent` is called, it resets the value of the agent to the provided state and takes away the agent's failure state so the agent can accept new actions. If the `:clear-actions true` option is provided, the agent's action queue is cleared; otherwise, pending actions will be called sequentially. `restart-agent` returns the new state of the agent.

To reset the agent in the preceding example:

```
user=> (restart-agent my-agent 5 :clear-actions true)
5
```

And now, the agent can be sent more actions:

```
user=> (send my-agent + 1)
#<Agent@1365360: 5>
user=> @my-agent
6
```

Waiting for Agents

Although agents are by their nature asynchronous, it is occasionally necessary to force a certain degree of synchronicity. For example, if a long-running action is being performed on an agent, a result might be required in the original thread before computation can continue. For this purpose, Clojure provides the `await` and `await-for` functions, both of which block a thread until an agent has finished processing its actions.

`await` takes any number of agents as its arguments and blocks the current thread indefinitely until all actions to the provided agent(s) which were dispatched from the current thread) are complete. It always returns nil.

`await-for` is nearly identical, except that it takes a timeout (in milliseconds) as its first argument and any number of agents as additional arguments. If the timeout expires before all the agents are finished, `await-for` returns nil. If the agents did finish before the timeout, it returns a non-nil value.

Shutting Down Agents

Whenever agents are used in a Clojure program, the Clojure runtime creates a thread pool in which to run agent actions behind the scenes. Normally, it isn't necessary to concern yourself about this, except that a Java/Clojure program will not gracefully terminate while there is still an active thread pool. To deactivate the agent thread pool, call the `shutdown-agents` function with no arguments. All currently running actions will complete, but no more will actions to agents will be accepted, and when all actions are complete the pool will shut down, allowing the program to terminate.

Never call `shutdown-agents` unless you intend to terminate the running program. `shutdown-agents` is irreversible without restarting your application, and after calling it agents can no longer be updated: all calls to send or send-off will throw exceptions.

When to Use Agents

When deciding when to use agents, it is very important to realize that agents are not only a means of managing state, but also managing program execution. Using agents doesn't just imply managed state with identities, but also splitting up computational processes across multiple threads.

As state management tools, agents are effective although they don't have all the features that refs do, such as transactions and ensuring data consistency. They are an uncoordinated identity type. For data that really needs these things, definitely consider using refs. Likewise, agents don't offer much more than atoms for simple uncoordinated state management. If all you need to do is ensure the integrity of individual pieces of state, atoms are probably a better choice than agents.

The important feature of agents is not only that they protect state, but that updates to that state occur *concurrently* with the thread that initiated the update. If, as in the previous examples, the only action functions being passed to agents are simple and blindingly fast, like +, there isn't much benefit to using an agent. But when the functions are more processing intensive, or when they perform IO (something that isn't even possible within transactions), there can be huge benefit to having it occur out-of-band. Every action function passed to an agent is offloaded from the calling thread, freeing it up for other important tasks.

This concurrency is the most important feature of agents. Their state management is convenient and works very well in concert with the concurrency features, but concurrency is the primary motivation behind choosing agents as opposed to one of Clojure's other identity types.

Vars and Thread-Local State

In addition to refs, atoms, and agents, Clojure has a fourth way of "changing" state: thread local var bindings. Since they are thread-local, they're not useful for shared access to state from different threads.

Rather, vars are ordinary bindings (the same ones discussed in Chapter 1, those created by def) which can be rebound on a per-thread basis and obey stack discipline. This allows for some level of imperative-style coding. I=It's the only way in Clojure to "change" a variable other than using a full-blown reference type.

To establish a thread-local binding for a var, use the binding form. binding takes a vector of bindings and one or more body expressions. The binding vector consists of a series of pairs of symbols and values. Then, the body expressions are evaluated within an implicit do, using the provided values whenever their matching symbols are encountered. binding may only be used on vars which are already defined by def on the top level. For example, the following code:

```
user=> (def x 5)
#'user/x
user=> (def y 3)
#'user/y
user=> (binding [x 2 y 1] (+ x y))
3
user=> (+ x y)
8
```

Within the context of the binding expression, (+ x y) yields 3. Outside the binding expression, (+ x y) uses the original values of the vars, yielding 8.

So far, binding might just look similar to let. The difference is, rather than establishing a local symbol, it actually rebinds it for all uses, so long as it's used at a lower position within the same call stack. For example, consider the following REPL session:

```
user=> (def x 5)
#'user/x
user=> (def y 3)
#'user/y
user=> (defn get-val [] (+ x y))
#'user/get-val
user=> (get-val)
8
user=> (binding [x 1 y 2] (get-val))
3
```

Binding actually reestablishes the values of x and y for all uses. When the get-val function is used within the stack context of the binding form, it picks up on the thread-local bindings of x and y established by binding and uses them.

Additionally, symbol bindings established by binding can be updated using the set! function, similar to imperative variables in most other programming languages. The following example is lengthy, but it demonstrates how independent code can update the same binding:

```
user=> (def x 5)
#'user/x
user=> (def y 3)
#'user/y
user=> (defn set-val [] (set! x 10))
#'user/set-val
user=> (defn get-val [] (+ x y))
#'user/get-val
 user=> (binding [x 1 y 2] (set-val) (get-val))
12
```

Notice how set-val was called first, and resets the value of x to 10, so that when get-val comes along later, it uses the updated value. Within the binding form, all references to bound symbols will see changes made by set!, just as if, for that limited context, they were ordinary, imperative, mutable variables.

When to Use Thread-Local Vars

There are very few cases where it is appropriate to use thread-local state in Clojure. Extensive use of it goes against the spirit of functional programming, and is it only provided as a concession to the very few cases where it is necessary for performance or practicality.

Scenarios where thread-local vars are useful tend to fall into two categories:

- Algorithms where it is much more logical and convenient to keep track of some state as a mutable variable. Examples include some parsers and state machines. Usually, however, an equivalent, purely functional algorithm *does* exist, even if it's not apparent to a programmer from an imperative background.

- Places where the semantics truly indicate a thread-local, context-based value that can be changed, such as a settings toggle. For example, many of Clojure's runtime settings are stored in var bindings, where they are easily accessible from all code and can be set! to new values conveniently. One example is *out*, which points to the standard output stream.

Keeping Track of Identities

There is more to managing state than just updating it, and so Clojure provides two very useful "hooks" into its state management system, which make it easy to write code that keeps track of states and identities.

Validators

Validators are functions that can be attached to any state type (refs, atoms, agents, and vars) and which validate any update before it is committed as the new value of the identity. If a new value is not approved by the validator function, the state of the identity is not changed.

To add a validator to an identity, use the set-validator! function. It takes two arguments: an identity and a function. The function must not have side effects, must take a single argument, and must return a boolean.

Then, whenever the state of the identity is about to be updated, the provided validator function will be passed the new value of the identity. If it returns true, the identity is updated normally. If it returns false or throws an exception, an exception is thrown from the identity update function.

For example, the following code sets a validator on a ref, ensuring that all values must be greater than zero:

```
user=> (def my-ref (ref 5))
#'user/my-ref
user=> (set-validator! my-ref (fn [x] (< 0 x)))
nil
user=> (dosync (alter my-ref - 10))
#<CompilerException java.lang.IllegalStateException: Invalid Reference State>
user=> (dosync (alter my-ref - 10) (alter my-ref + 15))
10
user=> @my-ref
5
```

And on an agent:

```
user=> (def my-agent (agent 5))
#'user/my-agent
user=> (set-validator! my-agent (fn [x] (< 0 x)))
nil
user=> (send my-agent - 10)
#<Agent 5>
user=> (agent-errors my-agent)
(#<CompilerException java.lang.IllegalStateException: Invalid Reference State>)
```

Note that on agents, the error is trapped and logged using the agent error-handling system, rather than being thrown immediately as it is with refs.

If the value of an identity is *already* invalid according to the given validator function when setting a validator, an exception is thrown and the validator is not set:

```
user=> (def my-atom (atom -5))
#'user/my-atom
```

```
user=> (set-validator! my-atom (fn [x] (< 0 x)))
#<CompilerException java.lang.RuntimeException java.lang.IllegalStateException: Invalid
Reference State>
```

The current validator function for an identity may be retrieved using the get-validator function, which takes a single identity as an argument:

```
user=> (def my-agent (agent 5))
#'user/my-agent
user=> (get-validator my-agent)
#<user$eval__4868$fn__4870 user$eval__4868$fn_4870@1dc518b>
```

As can be seen, the string representation of a function isn't very useful. However, since functions are first-class entities in Clojure, you can use the returned function however you wish—use it as a validator on another identity, call it with a value to see what it returns, or anything.

To remove a validator, just pass nil instead of a validator function to set-validator!

Watches

Watches are functions which are called whenever a state changes. They work on refs, atoms, agents, and vars (although with vars, they are only called with root binding changes, not when updated with set!).

Unlike validators, they are called immediately after the state has changed (for agents, this is in the same thread). Each identity may have multiple watches: each watch has an arbitrary key that can be used to identify it later. Watches are useful for structuring program flow that logically depends on the value of an identity—they easily provide a form of event-based or reactive programming.

To add a watch, use the add-watch function. It takes three arguments: an identity, a key, and a function. The key may be any value, provided it is unique among an identity's watchers.

The watch function itself takes four arguments: the key, the identity, the old state of the identity, and the new state.

For example, the following code uses watches to print the old and new values of a ref whenever it is updated:

```
user=> (defn my-watch [key identity old-val new-val]
                 (println (str "Old: " old-val))
                 (println (str "New: " new-val)))
#'user/my-watch
user=> (def my-ref (ref 5))
#'user/my-ref
user=> (add-watch my-ref "watch1" my-watch)
#<Ref 5>
user=> (dosync (alter my-ref inc))
Old: 5
```

```
New: 6
6
```

Note that if an identity is being updated in rapid succession, it may have been updated again by the time the first watch function is called. This is why watch functions are passed the old and new value of the identity: they reflect the state change from the update that actually triggered the watch. Dereferencing the identity within the watch function may yield a different value than the new value passed in if there are a lot of updates occurring.

To remove a watch, use the `remove-watch` function. It is very simple: it just takes an identity and a key, and removes watchers associated with that key from the identity.

```
user=> (remove-watch my-ref "watch1")
#<Ref 6>
```

Summary

Clojure's state management systems provide an array of effective ways to manage state. They combine a more sophisticated philosophical approach to state with state-of-the-art Software Transactional Memory and agent-based systems to make state management clean and effective to use. Managing state in Clojure is usually much less error prone than in other languages and works the same in single or multithreaded programs. With four distinct tools state management strategies, there should always be something that meets your needs:

- Use refs provide synchronous, coordinated updates, and allow direct access to the STM system.

- Use atoms to manage synchronous, independent state (such as cached or memorized values) with maximum efficiency.

- Use agents to manage asynchronous state as well as introduce concurrency into your program.

- Use vars to maintain state within a stack discipline to efficiently simulate mutable variables for algorithms that require it.

- Use validator functions to maintain data integrity.

- Use watches to trigger events dependent on an identity's values.

CHAPTER 7

■ ■ ■

Namespaces and Libraries

Organizing Clojure Code

Namespaces are the means by which you divide your Clojure code into logical groups, similar to packages in Java or modules in other languages. Almost every Clojure source file begins with a *namespace declaration* using the **ns** macro. The following code is an example of a namespace declaration:

```
(ns clojure.contrib.gen-html-docs
  (:require [clojure.contrib.duck-streams :as duck-streams])
  (:use (clojure.contrib seq-utils str-utils repl-utils def prxml))
  (:import (java.lang Exception)
           (java.util.regex Pattern)))
```

Fundamentally, a namespace is just a Clojure map. The keys of the map are Clojure symbols and the values are either Clojure Vars or Java classes. The Clojure compiler uses that map to figure out the meaning of each symbol in your source code. Special functions allow you to add, remove, or change entries in the namespace map.

Namespace Basics

The **ns** macro has dozens of options for configuring a namespace, so before tackling it you should understand the lower level functions on which it is based.

Switching Namespaces with in-ns

Whenever you are working at the Clojure REPL, the REPL prompt tells you that you are "in" a particular namespace. Clojure always starts in the **user** namespace:

```
user=>
```

Any symbols you define will be created in the **user** namespace. You can switch to a different namespace with the **in-ns** function:

```
user=> (in-ns 'greetings)
#<Namespace greetings>
greetings=>
```

in-ns takes a symbol argument, and switches to the namespace named by the symbol, creating it if it does not already exist. Please notice in the example that the symbol **greetings** was quoted to prevent Clojure from trying to evaluate it.

Referring to Other Namespaces

A newly-created namespace does not have any symbols in it, not even the core language functions. If you try to call a built-in Clojure function, you will get an error:

```
greetings=> (println "Hello, World!")
java.lang.Exception: Unable to resolve symbol: println in this context
```

Clojure's built-in functions are defined in the namespace **clojure.core**, and you can refer to them from your new namespace by *qualifying* the symbols with their namespace:

```
greetings=> (clojure.core/println "Hello, World!")
Hello, World!
nil
```

To avoid having to qualify all the symbols you use, you can *refer* another namespace with the **refer** function, which is also defined in **clojure.core**:

```
greetings=> (clojure.core/refer 'clojure.core)
nil
```

Now you can call functions in clojure.core directly, without qualification:

```
greetings=> (println "Hello, World!")
Hello, World!
nil
```

refer takes a symbol argument and maps all the *public* symbols from that namespace into the current namespace. (We will cover the difference between public and private symbols later in the section "Public and Private Vars.") The symbols are still mapped to the values in their original namespace. By calling **refer** in the example, you created a *namespace mapping* from the symbol **greetings/println** to the Var **#'clojure.core/println**.

refer takes additional options that specify *filters* for the symbols to be referred. The options take the form of a keyword followed by a list or map of symbols. The **:exclude** option is followed by a (quoted) list of symbols that should *not* be referred into the current namespace. For example, the following code:

```
(refer 'clojure.core :exclude '(map set))
```

This refers all the symbols in the **clojure.core** namespace, except **map** and **set**. You can then define your own versions of **map** and **set** that do not clash with the original definitions in **clojure.core**.

The **:only** option is also followed by a list of symbols, but it specifies that only the symbols in the list you specify should be referred into the current namespace. For example, the following code:

```
(refer 'clojure.core :only '(println prn))
```

This refers only the two symbols **println** and **prn** from **clojure.core**; other symbols in **clojure.core** must still be namespace-qualified, like **clojure.core/def**.

Lastly, **refer** allows you to rename some symbols when referring them, by including the **:rename** keyword followed by a map from symbols in the original namespace to symbols in the current namespace.

```
(refer 'clojure.core :rename {'map 'core-map, 'set 'core-set})
```

This refers all symbols from **clojure.core**, but makes the symbol **clojure.core/map** available in the current namespace as **core-map** and **clojure.core/set** available as **core-set**. This might be useful if you want to define your own version of a built-in function that calls the original version.

As an alternative to copying the mappings from one namespace, you can create a local *alias* to another namespace, so you can refer to it by a shorter name. Namespace aliases are created with the **alias** function:

```
(alias local-name namespace-name)
```

The arguments **local-name** and **namespace-name** are both (quoted) symbols. **alias** creates an alias in the current namespace to the named namespace. After calling **alias**, you can reference symbols in the other namespace using **local-name**, instead of the full namespace name. For example, the following code:

```
greetings> (alias 'set 'clojure.set)
nil
greetings> (set/union #{1 3 5} #{2 3 4})
#{1 2 3 4 5}
```

Loading Other Namespaces

refer and **alias** allow you to reference symbols in namespaces that already exist. But what about namespaces defined in other files, including files that haven't been loaded yet? Clojure provides a variety of functions for loading code from files.

Loading from a File or Stream

The simplest load function is **load-file**:

```
(load-file name)
```

load-file takes one argument, a file name, and attempts to read and evaluate every Clojure form in the file. The file name is given as a String, including any directories, and is interpreted in the context of the current working directory (the directory in which you started Clojure). On a Unix-like system, it might look like the following:

```
(load-file "path/to/file.clj")
```

On Windows, back-slashes must be escaped, because the file name is a String:

```
(load-file "C:\\Documents\\file.clj")
```

If you want to load code from some other source, such as a network connection, you can use the **load-reader** function, which takes a **java.io.Reader** as its argument, and reads and evaluates code from the **Reader**.

Loading from the Classpath

The Java Virtual Machine uses a special variable called the *classpath*, a list of directories from which to load executable code. Clojure programs also use the classpath to search for source files.

The classpath is normally specified on the Java command line as a set of directories and JAR files. The following example, for Unix-like systems, creates a classpath consisting of the Clojure JAR and the /code/sources directory.

```
java -cp clojure.jar:/code/sources clojure.main
```

Java development environments and build-management tools usually have their own methods for configuring the classpath; consult your tools' documentation for more information.

Namespace Names vs. File Names

Clojure namespaces follow similar naming conventions to Java packages: they are organized hierarchically with parts separated by periods. A popular convention is to name your libraries using the reversed form of an Internet domain name that you control. So if you work for www.example.com, your namespaces might be named com.example.one, com.example.two, and so on.

When translating between namespace names and file names, periods become directory separators and hyphens become underscores. So, on Unix-like systems, the Clojure namespace **com.example.my-cool-library** would be defined in the file **com/example/my_cool_library.clj**. In order to load the namespace, the directory containing **com** must be on the classpath.

Loading Resources from the Classpath

The **load** function takes any number of String arguments, each of which names a *resource* on the classpath. A resource name is like a file name, but without the **.clj** extension. If the resource name begins with a forward slash (/), it is interpreted as being in some directory on the classpath. For example, the following code:

```
(load "/com/example/my_library")
```

This call will search each location on the classpath for the file **com/example/my_library.clj**. (It will also search for the precompiled class file **com/example/my_library.class**. Compilation will be covered in Chapter 10.)

If an argument to **load** does not begin with a slash, it is interpreted as being relative to the directory of the current namespace.

```
greetings=> (load "hello")
```

This call to **load**, from within the **greetings** namespace, will search the classpath for the file **greetings/hello.clj**.

Loading Namespaces from the Classpath

You will rarely use the **load** function in normal code. Instead, Clojure provides two higher level functions, **require** and **use**, to load namespaces.

The **require** function takes any number of arguments, each of which is a symbol, a vector *libspec*, a *prefix list*, or a *flag*. Arguments are typically quoted to prevent evaluation. The simplest case, a symbol, converts the symbol to a file name, searches the classpath for that file, loads it, and verifies that a namespace with the given name was, in fact, created.

```
(require 'com.example.lib)
```

This loads the file **com/example/lib.clj** from the classpath. After loading the file, if the namespace **com.example.lib** does not exist, **require** will throw an exception. If the namespace has already been loaded, **require** will ignore it.

A *libspec* argument to **require** allows you to specify options for loading the namespace. It takes the form of a vector, starting with a symbol, followed by keyword options. The only option it accepts (for now) is **:as**, which creates a local alias to the namespace.

```
(require '[com.example.lib :as lib])
```

This loads the namespace **com.example.lib** and aliases it as **lib** in the current namespace.

Often several namespaces share a common prefix. In that case, you can use *prefix lists* to load several namespaces. A prefix list is a list starting with the symbol shared by all the namespaces, followed by the remaining parts of each namespace name. For example, instead of writing:

```
(require 'com.example.one 'com.example.two 'com.example.three)
```

You can write this equivalent:

```
(require '(com.example one two three))
```

Prefix lists and libspecs can be combined, as in this example:

```
(require '(com.example one [two :as t]))
```

This loads the namespaces **com.example.one** and **com.example.two**, and creates an alias **t** for **com.example.two**.

Lastly, the **require** function accepts any number of *flags*, given as keywords anywhere in its arguments. The **:reload** flag causes **require** to load all namespaces in the arguments, even if they have already been loaded. For example, the following code:

```
(require 'com.example.one 'com.example.two :reload)
```

Another flag, **:reload-all**, will reload the listed namespaces *and* all dependent namespaces **require**'d by those namespaces. The **:reload** and **:reload-all** flags are useful when you are experimenting at the REPL and want to load changes you have made in your source files.

The **:verbose** flag prints debugging information about the lower-level function calls being made by **require**.

```
user=> (require '(clojure zip [set :as s]) :verbose)
(clojure.core/load "/clojure/zip")
(clojure.core/load "/clojure/set")
(clojure.core/in-ns 'user)
(clojure.core/alias 's 'clojure.set)
nil
```

Loading and Referring Namespaces in One Step

Frequently, you may want to **require** a namespace and also **refer** certain symbols in it. The **use** function makes this a one-step operation. Calling **use** is equivalent to calling **require** and then **refer**. **use** accepts the **:reload**, **:reload-all**, and **:verbose** flags of **require**; and also the **:exclude**, **:only**, and **:rename** options of **refer**, grouped in a vector with the namespace they affect. For example, see the following line of code:

```
(use '[com.example.library :only (a b c)] :reload-all :verbose)
```

This (re)loads the namespace **com.example.library** and refers the three symbols **a**, **b**, and **c** into the current namespace. Note that you do not need to quote the list **(a b c)** because the entire vector is already quoted.

■ **Caution** Except when experimenting at the REPL, it is almost always a bad idea to **use** a namespace without limiting the symbols it refers with **:only**. Calling **use** without **:only** makes it impossible for readers of your code to know where a particular symbol comes from and can also lead to unexpected name clashes if the **use**'d namespace changes.

Importing Java Classes

The last namespace function deals with Java classes. You can always refer to a Java class by its fully-qualified name, such as **java.util.Date**. To refer to a class without its package, you can *import* it.

```
user=> (import 'java.util.Date) nil
user=> (new Date)
#<Date Fri Oct 23 16:31:28 EDT 2009>
```

In Clojure 1.0, **import** is a function, so you must quote its arguments, as in the example. Starting with Clojure 1.1, **import** is a macro, and its arguments do not need to be quoted. **import** also accepts prefix lists similar to **require** and **use**. The prefix must be a complete Java package name; the class name may not contain periods.

```
(import '(java.util.regex Pattern Matcher))
```

As a special case, nested Java classes (sometimes called "inner classes") must be imported using their *binary class name*, which the JVM uses internally. The binary class name of an inner class consists of the outer class name, followed by a $ sign, followed by the inner class name. For example, the binary name of a class **Wheel** nested inside a class **Truck** is **Truck$Wheel**.

In Clojure, a nested Java class cannot be named without its enclosing class. For example, to import the nested class **javax.swing.Box.Filler**, you must do this:

```
(import '(javax.swing Box$Filler))
```

After that import, you can refer to the class as **Box$Filler**.

Bringing It All Together: Namespace Declarations

When writing normal Clojure code, you will not call the **in-ns**, **refer**, **alias**, **load**, **require**, **use**, and **import** functions directly. Instead, you will typically start your Clojure source file with a *namespace declaration* using the **ns** macro, like the example at the start of this chapter.

```
(ns name & references)
```

The **ns** macro takes a symbol as its first argument; it creates a new namespace with that name and sets it to be the current namespace. Because **ns** is a macro that does not evaluate its arguments, the name does not need to be quoted.

The remaining arguments to the ns macro take the same form as the **refer**, **load**, **require**, **use**, and **import** functions, with two differences:

- Arguments are never quoted.

- The function name is given as a keyword.

Here's an example.

```
(ns com.example.library
  (:require [clojure.contrib.sql :as sql])
  (:use (com.example one two))
  (:import (java.util Date Calendar)
           (java.io File FileInputStream)))
```

This creates a new namespace, **com.example.library**, and automatically refers the **clojure.core** namespace. It loads the **clojure.contrib.sql** namespace and aliases it as **sql**. It loads the namespaces **com.example.one** and **com.example.two** and refers all the symbols from them into the current namespace. Finally, it imports the Java classes **Date**, **Calendar**, **File**, and **FileInputStream**.

Unlike the **in-ns** function, the **ns** macro automatically refers the **clojure.core** namespace, as previously mentioned. If you want to control which core symbols get referred in your namespace, use the **:refer-clojure** argument to **ns**, like this:

```
(ns com.example.library
  (:refer-clojure :exclude (map set)))
```

The **:refer-clojure** form takes the same arguments that you would use with **(refer 'clojure.core)**. If you don't want any symbols referred from **clojure.core**, you can pass an empty list to **:only**, like **(:refer-clojure :only ())**.

Symbols and Namespaces

As previously mentioned, namespaces are essentially maps from symbols to Vars, but they have a few unique properties. Symbols can have properties that tie them to specific namespaces.

Namespace Metadata

Like most Clojure objects, namespaces can have metadata (see Chapter 8) attached to them. You can add metadata to the namespace by placing read-time metadata on the symbol in the ns macro, like this:

```
(ns #^{:doc "This is my great library."
       :author "Mr. Quux <quux@example.com>"
   com.example.my-great-library)
```

While Clojure does not specify any "official" metadata keys for namespaces (like **:tag** and **:arglists** for functions) many Clojure library developers have adopted the convention of using **:doc** metadata to describe the general purpose of a namespace and **:author** metadata for the author's name and e-mail address.

Forward Declarations

The Clojure compiler requires that symbols be defined before they are used. Usually this leads to organizing your source files with simple, low-level functions at the top and more complex functions at the bottom. But sometimes, you need to use a symbol before it can be defined. To prevent the compiler from throwing an Exception, you must use a *forward declaration*.

(declare & *symbols*)

A forward declaration is created with the **declare** macro, which simply tells the compiler, "This symbol exists, it will be defined later." Here is a contrived, and very inefficient, example:

```
(declare is-even? is-odd?)

(defn is-even? [n]
  (if (= n 2) true
    (is-odd? (dec n))))

(defn is-odd? [n]
  (if (= n 3) true
    (is-even? (dec n))))
```

Namespace-Qualified Symbols and Keywords .

As you saw earlier, symbols can be *qualified* with a namespace. The functions **name** and **namespace** return the strings representing each part of the symbol:

```
user=> (name 'com.example/thing)
"thing"
user=> (namespace 'com.example/thing)
"com.example"
```

Notice that the symbol is *quoted* to prevent Clojure from trying to resolve it as a class or Var.
The **namespace** function returns **nil** for *unqualified* symbols, which have no namespace:

```
user=> (namespace 'stuff)
nil
```

Keywords, too, can be namespace-qualified; the **name** and **namespace** functions work as on symbols:

```
user=> (name :com.example/mykey)
"mykey"
user=> (namespace :com.example/mykey)
"com.example"
user=> (namespace :unqualified)
nil
```

As a syntactic convenience, you can create keywords in the current namespace by preceding their names with two colons instead of one. In the "user" namespace, the keyword `::thing` expands to `:user/thing`.

```
user=> (namespace ::keyword)
"user"
```

Although not explicitly for this purpose, the backquote ` reader macro can be used to create qualified symbols in the current namespace:

```
user=> `sym
user/sym
```

Constructing Symbols and Keywords

The **name** and **namespace** functions convert from symbols or keywords to strings. The **symbol** and **keyword** functions go the other way: given Strings for the name and, optionally, a namespace, they construct a symbol or keyword.

```
user=> (symbol "hello")
hello
user=> (symbol "com.example" "hello")
com.example/hello
user=> (keyword "thing")
:thing
user=> (keyword "user" "goodbye")
:user/goodbye
```

Note that the name given to the **keyword** function does not include the leading colon.

Public and Private Vars

By default, all definitions in a namespace are *public*, meaning they can be referenced from other namespaces and copied with **refer** or **use**. But many namespaces can be divided into two parts: one set of "internal" functions that should never be called from any other namespace and another set of "public" functions meant for use by other namespaces. These correspond, loosely, to the private and public methods of object-oriented languages like Java.

Private Vars in Clojure will never be copied by **refer** or **use**, and they cannot be referenced with a namespace-qualified symbol. In effect, they can only be used in the namespace in which they were defined.

There are two ways to create a private Var. The first is the **defn-** macro, which works exactly like **defn** but creates a private function definition. The second, which works for any definition, is to add **:private** metadata to the symbol you are defining.

```
(def #^{:private true} *my-private-value* 123)
```

Note that private Vars are never truly hidden; any code can get the value of the Var with **(deref (var namespace/name))**. But private Vars prevent you from inadvertently calling a function that you did not mean to be used by other parts of your application.

Advanced Namespace Operations

Unlike Java packages, which are simply a naming device, Clojure namespaces are first-class objects, with dedicated functions to query and manipulate them.

Querying Namespaces

The special Var ***ns*** is always bound to the current namespace. It is changed with **in-ns**.
The function **all-ns** takes no arguments and returns a sequence of all namespaces currently defined.

■ **Note** The set of namespaces is global; you cannot have multiple "instances" of Clojure loading different namespaces in the same JVM. It doesn't really make sense to talk about an "instance" of Clojure, since Clojure is just a compiler, not an interpreter like Jython or JRuby. You *can* create independent execution contexts using Java classloaders, an advanced Java topic outside the scope of this book.

Two functions help you get from a symbol naming a namespace to the namespace object itself. The **find-ns** function takes a symbol argument and returns the namespace with that name; or **nil** if no such namespace exists.

Often, you don't care if you're dealing with a namespace object directly or just the symbol naming it. For this purpose, a function called **the-ns** will accept either a namespace object, in which case it just returns the namespace; or a symbol, in which case it calls **find-ns**. Unlike **find-ns**, **the-ns** throws an Exception if the namespace does not exist. Most of the functions in this section call **the-ns** on their argument, so they may be called with either a namespace object (such as ***ns***) or a quoted symbol.

The **ns-name** function returns the name of a namespace as a symbol.

The **ns-aliases** function returns a map, from symbols to namespaces, representing all the namespace aliases defined in a namespace.

The **ns-map** function returns a map, from symbols to objects (Vars or classes), representing all the mappings in a namespace. Usually, this is more information than you want, so Clojure provides several auxiliary functions that return a subset of the mappings for a namespace. **ns-publics** returns mappings for all public Vars; **ns-interns** returns mappings for all Vars (both public and private); **ns-refers** returns mappings for all symbols referred from other namespaces; and **ns-imports** returns mappings for all Java classes.

For example, to get a list of all the public symbols in the **clojure.core** namespace, you can run:

```
(keys (ns-publics 'clojure.core))
```

Finally, you may want to find out what a symbol will resolve to when it is encountered in a particular context. The **ns-resolve** function takes a namespace and a symbol, and returns the Var or class to which that symbol is mapped in the namespace. For example, **clojure.core** imports the **java.math.BigDecimal** class, which you can discover by calling:

```
user> (ns-resolve 'clojure.core 'BigDecimal)
java.math.BigDecimal
```

As a shortcut, the **resolve** function is equivalent to **ns-resolve** for the current namespace.

Manipulating Namespaces

The **in-ns** function and **ns** macro both create a namespace and make it the current namespace. Likewise, **def** and its relatives all operate in the current namespace. There are some special cases, like code generation, where you want to create a namespace and define things in it without switching to it. You may be tempted to write something like this:

```
;; Bad code!
(let [original (ns-name *ns*)]
  (ns other)
  (defn f [] (println "Function f")
  (in-ns original)))
```

That won't work, because Clojure reads the symbol **f** in the current namespace *before* evaluating the **ns** form. You'll end up with **f** defined in the current namespace, not the **other** namespace.

Instead, you can use the **create-ns** function, which takes a symbol argument and returns a new namespace with that name (or returns an existing namespace with that name). Then you can use the **intern** function to define Vars in that namespace. Here's a version of the previous example that actually works:

```
(let [other-ns (create-ns 'other)]
  (intern other-ns 'f
          (fn [] (println "Function f")))))
```

The act of creating a Var and mapping it to a symbol in a namespace is called *interning* the Var, and that's exactly what the **intern** function does.

```
(intern namespace symbol value)
```

The value is optional; if it is omitted, the Var is created with no root value, similar to a forward declaration. The symbol must be a *bare* symbol, that is, without a namespace-qualifying prefix. The namespace argument may be either a symbol or a namespace.

The **ns-unmap** function is the opposite of **intern**; it removes a mapping from a namespace. For example, every Clojure namespace, regardless of how it is created, starts with mappings for all the classes in the `java.lang` package. If you wanted a completely empty namespace, you could create one like this:

```
(let [empty-ns (create-ns 'empty)]
  (doseq [sym (keys (ns-map empty-ns))]
    (ns-unmap empty-ns sym))
  empty-ns)
```

Finally, the `remove-ns` function will delete a namespace entirely, including all the Vars interned in it. Note that code in other namespaces may still hold references to those Vars in closures, but the Vars themselves are cleared, so any attempt to use them will throw an "unbound Var" Exception.

Namespaces As References

As I said at the beginning of the chapter, a namespace is basically a map from symbols to Vars or classes. It would be more accurate to say it is a *reference* to a map, because namespaces are mutable. All operations on namespaces are *atomic*, like Clojure Atoms. For example, if you redefine an existing function with `defn`, Clojure guarantees that the old and new definitions will never "overlap."

However, Clojure does not provide a way to *coordinate* namespace operations the way you can with Refs. If you redefine several functions, Clojure cannot guarantee that the "new" functions will all be updated at the same time. There may be a short time in which both old and new definitions are present.

In general, the problem of "hot-swapping" entire modules in a running program is very difficult, and requires support at the deepest levels of the language. Erlang, for example, is designed to support hot-swapping of modules. Java does not have built-in support for hot-swapping, although some Java application servers attempt to provide it.

Summary

There's a lot you can do with namespaces, and they may seem overwhelming at first. But in normal, day-to-day coding you only need a few features and conventions.

First, start every source file with a namespace declaration using `ns`, using `:import` and `:use` expressions to describe the classes and namespaces it depends on. Always use the `:only` option of `:use` to make it clear which symbols you need from the other namespace. Here is a complete example:

```
(ns com.example.apps.awesome
  (:use [clojure.set :only (union intersection)]
        [com.example.library :only (foo bar baz)]
        [com.example.logger :only (log)])
  (:import (java.io File InputStream OutputStream)
           (java.util Date)))
```

Don't be afraid to reuse good names just because they are part of `clojure.core`. Add the `:refer-clojure` expression to `ns` if needed.

Structure your source files to avoid the need for forward declarations. This usually means placing "primitive" definitions near the top and the "composite" definitions that depend on them toward the bottom.

CHAPTER 8

■ ■ ■

Metadata

Describing Your Code, in Code

Programmers often talk about metadata, or data about data. The definition of metadata varies in different contexts. Clojure provides mechanisms to attach metadata to objects, but it has a very specific definition: *metadata is a map of data attached to an object that does not affect the value of the object.*

Two objects with the same value and different metadata are considered equal (and have the same hash code). However, metadata has the same immutable semantics as Clojure's other data structures; modifying an object's metadata yields a *new* object, with the same value (and the same hash code) as the original object.

When updating a value, some operations preserve metadata and some do not, which this chapter discusses.

Reading and Writing Metadata

By default, metadata is not printed at the REPL. You can change this by setting ***print-meta*** to true, as we did for all the examples in this chapter.

```
(set! *print-meta* true)
```

You can attach metadata to a symbol or any of Clojure's built-in data structures with the **with-meta** function, and retrieve it using the **meta** function:

```
(with-meta obj meta-map)
(meta obj)
```

with-meta returns a new object, with the same value as **obj**, that has **meta-map** as its metadata. **meta** returns the metadata map of **obj**. For example, the following code:

```
user=> (with-meta [1 2] {:about "A vector"})
#^{:about "A vector"} [1 2]
```

You can also modify the metadata map of an object with the **vary-meta** function:

```
(vary-meta obj function & args)
```

vary-meta takes a function and applies it to the current metadata map of the object plus any arguments. It returns a new object with the updated metadata. For example, the following code:

```
user=> (def x (with-meta [3 4] {:help "Small vector"}))
user=> x
#^{:help "Small vector"} [3 4]
user=> (vary-meta x assoc :help "Tiny vector")
#^{:help "Tiny vector"} [3 4]
```

Notice that two objects with the same value and different metadata are equal (tested with Clojure's = function), but they are not the same object in memory (tested with Clojure's **identical?** function):

```
user=> (def v [1 2 3])
user=> (= v (with-meta v {:x 1}))
true
user=> (identical? v (with-meta v {:x 1}))
false
```

Also, note that you can only add metadata to Clojure-specific types such as lists, vectors, maps, and symbols (and functions in Clojure 1.2). Java classes, such as String and Number, do not support metadata.[1]

Metadata-Preserving Operations

Some operations that "modify" an immutable data structure preserve its metadata, others do not. For example, **conj** on a list preserves its metadata, but **cons** does not:

```
user=> (def x (with-meta (list 1 2) {:m 1}))
user=> x
#^{:m 1} (1 2)
user=> (conj x 3)
#^{:m 1} (3 1 2)
user=> (cons 3 x)
(3 1 2)  ;; no metadata!
```

In general, collection functions (conj, assoc, dissoc, and so on) are supposed to preserve metadata, while sequence functions (cons, take, drop, etc.) are not. But there are exceptions. In Clojure 1.0, **conj** on a vector does not preserve metadata (this is a bug) but in Clojure 1.1 it does. The moral is this: be careful with operations on data structures that have metadata, and don't assume that metadata will be preserved. Always test first.

---

[1] Why not? Conceivably, metadata could be stored in a global hash table, allowing metadata to be attached to arbitrary Java objects. However, this design has serious drawbacks with regard to performance and memory usage, so it is not supported.

■ **Caution** Metadata is quite an unusual feature of Clojure; few programming languages have anything like it. Whenever you consider using metadata, think very carefully about its semantics: metadata is *not part of the value of an object*. In general, any data that is relevant to users of your application should not be considered metadata. Metadata is information that only you, the programmer, care about.

Read-Time Metadata

The Clojure reader (described in Chapter 2) allows you to attach metadata to forms as they are read using the #^ reader macro. #^ is followed by a map of metadata, which will be attached to the next form read. When ***print-meta*** is true, Clojure prints metadata using the same syntax. For example, you can attach metadata to a literal vector like this:

```
user=> #^{:m 1} [1 2]
#^{:m 1} [1 2]
```

However, be very careful: #^ is not a substitute for **with-meta**! #^ attaches metadata to *literal forms*. Consider the following:

```
user=> #^{:m 1} (list 1 2)
(1 2)    ;; no metadata!
```

In this example, the #^ reader macro attaches the metadata map **{:m 1}** to the literal form **(list 1 2)**. When that form is evaluated, it returns the list **(1 2)** with no metadata.

The #^ reader macro is normally used to attach metadata to symbols, not data structures. Special forms such as **def** can make use of this read-time metadata (see the following section).

■ **Note** Clojure 1.0 provided the ^ reader macro as a shortcut for meta. However, this shortcut was not very useful and is deprecated in Clojure 1.1. Clojure 1.2 uses ^ in place of #^ for setting read-time metadata.

Metadata on Vars

The most common use of metadata in Clojure is to attach descriptive information to Vars. The **def**, **defn**, and **defmacro** forms attach some default metadata to every Var. For example, the following code:

```
user=> (meta (var or))
{:ns #<Namespace clojure.core>
 :name or
 :file "clojure/core.clj"
 :line 504
 :doc "Evaluates exprs one at a time..."
 :arglists ([] [x] [x & next])
 :macro true}
```

In addition, **def** and its kin will copy metadata from the symbol used to name the Var onto the Var itself. Combined with the **#^** reader macro, this provides a convenient way to attach metadata to Vars when they are created:

```
user=> (def #^{:doc "My cool thing"} *thing*)
#'user/*thing*
user=> (:doc (meta (var *thing*)))
"My cool thing"
```

Clojure's **doc** macro uses a Var's **:doc** and **:arglists** metadata to print a description of it:

```
user=> (doc *thing*)
-------------------------
user/*thing*
nil
  My cool thing
```

The documentation string in the **defn** and **defmacro** forms is automatically set as **:doc** metadata on the Var being defined. **defn** and **defmacro** also accept an optional metadata map between the documentation string and the parameter list:

```
(defn name doc-string meta-map [params] ...)
(defmacro name doc-string meta-map [params] ...)
```

Clojure uses several standard metadata keys for global Vars. These are described in Table 8-1. If you are adding application-specific metadata, it is recommended that you use namespace-qualified keywords, such as **:my-app/meta**, as keys to avoid potential name clashes.

Table 8-1. Standard Var Metadata

Metadata Key	Value	Type
:name	The Var's name	Symbol
:ns	The Var's namespace	Namespace
:file	File from which it was loaded	String
:line	Line on which it was defined	Integer
:doc	Documentation string	String
:arglists	Function/macro arguments	List of Vectors of Symbols
:macro	True for macros; false by default	Boolean
:private	True for private Vars, false by default	Boolean
:tag	Type of the value or function return value	Class or Symbol

Type Tags

The :**tag** metadata key is used to attach type "hints" to symbols and Vars. This helps the Clojure compiler optimize the bytecode it generates. Type hints are described in detail in Chapter 15.

Private Vars

As described in Chapter 7, Vars with :**private true** in their metadata are private. Private Vars cannot be referred from namespaces other than the one in which they were defined. The **defn-** macro creates private functions; to create private macros or other Vars, add metadata to the Var like this:

```
(def #^{:private true} *my-private-var*)  ;; for Vars
(defmacro my-private-macro {:private true} [args] ...)  ;; for macros
```

Metadata on Reference Types

Clojure's mutable reference types—Var, Ref, Agent, Atom, and also Namespaces—all support metadata. You can change the metadata map for any reference type with the **alter-meta!** function:

```
(alter-meta! iref f & args)
```

alter-meta! works like **alter** does for Refs; it calls function **f** on the current metadata map of **iref**, with addition arguments **args**. For example, you can add metadata to an existing Var like this:

```
user=> (alter-meta! (var for) assoc :note "Not a loop!")
{:note "Not a loop!", :macro true, ...
user=> (:note (meta (var for)))
"Not a loop!"
```

alter-meta! is an atomic operation, but it does not require a transaction like **alter**.
    The **ref**, **agent**, and **atom** functions accept a :**meta** option specifying an initial metadata map. For example, the following code:

```
user=> (def r (ref nil :meta {:about "This is my ref"}))
user=> (meta r)
{:about "This is my ref"}
```

Summary

Metadata is an unusual feature, not something you will make frequent use of in day-to-day programming. Many things that might be reasonably described as "metadata" within in application, such as timestamps or user names, turn out to be a bad fit for Clojure metadata. Metadata is most useful for *metaprogramming*, where it can describe one piece of code for use by another piece of code. In that sense, it fills a role similar to Java's annotations. The full capabilities of metadata are still being explored by Clojure programmers. Metadata already plays a role in the Clojure compiler (for type hinting) and that role will likely be expanded in future Clojure releases.

■ ■ ■

CHAPTER 9

Multimethods and Hierarchies

Runtime Polymorphism Without Classes

Clojure is not an object-oriented language in the traditional sense of classes and methods, although it is built on Java's object-oriented foundation.

Most mainstream object-oriented languages, such as Java and C++, use classes to define a tree-like hierarchy of types and to provide implementations of the methods supported by those types.

Clojure separates type hierarchies from method implementations, which greatly simplifies thorny issues such as multiple inheritance. In addition, it permits you to define multiple, independent hierarchies over the same types. This makes it possible to define IS-A relationships that more closely model the real world.

Multimethods

Clojure multimethods provide *runtime polymorphic dispatch*. That is, they permit you to define a function with multiple implementations. At runtime, the implementation that executes is determined based on the arguments to the function.

Most object-oriented languages have *single-argument, type-based dispatch*, meaning that the method to be run is determined solely by the type, or class, of the first argument. The method is called "on" that first argument. Both Java and C++ place that first argument before the method name to denote its special significance.

Clojure multimethods are more flexible. They support *multiple dispatch*, meaning the implementation can be determined by any and all arguments to the function. Also, the dispatch can be based on any feature of the arguments, not just type.

Multimethods are created with **defmulti** and implemented with **defmethod**.

```
(defmulti name dispatch-fn)
(defmethod multifn dispatch-value [args...] & body)
```

You call a multimethod like an ordinary function. When you call it, the dispatch function is immediately called with the same arguments that you gave to the multimethod. The value returned by the dispatch function is called the *dispatch value*. Clojure then searches for a method (defined with **defmethod**) with a matching dispatch value.

Suppose you are writing a fantasy role-playing game populated with different species of creatures: humans, elves, orcs, and so on. Each creature could be represented by a map, like the following:

```
(def a {:name "Arthur", :species ::human, :strength 8})
(def b {:name "Balfor", :species ::elf, :strength 7})
```

```
(def c {:name "Calis", :species ::elf, :strength 5})
(def d {:name "Drung", :species ::orc, :strength 6})
```

I used namespace-qualified keywords for species (::human instead of :human) for reasons that will be important later. (See Chapter 7 for an explanation of qualified keywords.)

Now you can define a multimethod that dispatches on the particular species of creature. For example, you can give each species a different style of movement:

```
(defmulti move :species)

(defmethod move ::elf [creature]
  (str (:name creature) " runs swiftly."))

(defmethod move ::human [creature]
  (str (:name creature) " walks steadily."))

(defmethod move ::orc [creature]
  (str (:name creature) " stomps heavily."))
```

When you call **move**, the appropriate method is invoked:

```
user=> (move a)
"Arthur walks steadily."
user=> (move b)
"Balfor runs swiftly."
user=> (move c)
"Calis runs swiftly."
```

What's happening here? When you call **(move a)**, Clojure first calls the dispatch function for the **move** multimethod, which you have defined to be the keyword **:species**. Remember that a keyword, called on a map, returns the value of that key in the map. So **(move a)** calls **(:species a)**, which returns **::human**. Clojure then searches for a method of **move** with the dispatch value **::human**, and invokes that method.

The same behavior could be implemented with a conditional. The advantage of the multimethod is that you can add new methods at any time. If you were to add a new species of creature, you could simply define another **move** method without changing any existing code.

The dispatch function doesn't have to be a simple keyword; it can be any arbitrary function. For example, you could use a dispatch function that categorizes creatures based on their strength:

```
(defmulti attack (fn [creature]
                   (if (> (:strength creature) 5)
                     :strong
                     :weak)))

(defmethod attack :strong [creature]
  (str (:name creature) " attacks mightily."))

(defmethod attack :weak [creature]
  (str (:name creature) " attacks feebly."))
```

When you call the **attack** multimethod, it first calls the anonymous **fn**, which returns either **:strong** or **:weak**. That keyword (the dispatch value) determines which attack method gets called:

```
user=> (attack c)
"Calis attacks feebly."
user=> (attack d)
"Drung attacks mightily."
```

Multiple Dispatch

As I said at the beginning of this chapter, multimethods support dispatching on multiple arguments. To do this, the dispatch function returns a vector. For example, in this game, you can define a multimethod that describes how two different creatures react when they meet. Let's say elves and orcs are enemies, but elves are friendly to one another:

```
(defmulti encounter (fn [x y]
                        [(:species x) (:species y)]))
(defmethod encounter [::elf ::orc] [elf orc]
  (str "Brave elf " (:name elf)
       " attacks evil orc " (:name orc)))
(defmethod encounter [::orc ::elf] [orc elf]
  (str "Evil orc " (:name orc)
       " attacks innocent elf " (:name elf)))
(defmethod encounter [::elf ::elf] [orc1 orc2]
  (str "Two elves, " (:name orc1)
       " and " (:name orc2)
       ", greet each other."))
```

Notice that the the method arguments do not have to have the same names as the multimethod's arguments, but the dispatch function and the methods must all accept the same *number* of arguments.

Now you can call the **encounter** multimethod on two creatures and see what happens:

```
user=> (encounter b c)
"Two elves, Balfor and Calis, greet each other."
user=> (encounter d b)
"Evil orc Drung attacks innocent elf Balfor"
```

Default Dispatch Values

Notice that you haven't defined **encounter** methods for all possible combinations of creatures. If you try to call **encounter** on an undefined combination, you get an error:

```
user=> (encounter a c)
java.lang.IllegalArgumentException:
No method in multimethod 'encounter'
for dispatch value: [:user/human :user/elf]
```

You could keep defining methods for each possible combination, but instead you can provide a default method implementation, which uses the keyword **:default** as the dispatch value.

```
(defmethod encounter :default [x y]
  (str (:name x) " and " (:name y)
       " ignore each other."))
```

The default method will be called when no other method matches:

```
user=> (encounter a c)
"Arthur and Calis ignore each other."
```

You can specify an alternate default dispatch value by adding the :default option to defmulti, like this:

```
(defmulti talk :species :default "other")
(defmethod talk ::orc [creature]
  (str (:name creature) " grunts."))
(defmethod talk "other" [creature]
  (str (:name creature) " speaks."))
```

Hierarchies

In most object-oriented languages, type hierarchies are implicitly defined by the inheritance relationships of classes and subclasses. Since classes also define method implementations, the relationships can get tricky rather quickly, especially in languages that permit multiple inheritance, such as C++. Java avoids that problem by disallowing multiple inheritance, but that in turn makes it harder to model some real-world problems.

In Clojure, type hierarchies are completely independent from method implementations, so they are more flexible than class-based inheritance. They can support almost any combination of relationships, including multiple inheritance and multiple roots.

Clojure defines one "global" hierarchy, which we will describe first. You can also create independent hierarchies, which will be covered at the end of this section.

(derive *child parent*)

derive creates an IS-A relationship between child and parent. The child and parent are referred to as *tags*, because they are used to identify a type or category. Tags may be either keywords or symbols, and (in the global hierarchy) must be namespace-qualified (see Chapter 7).

Continuing with your fantasy game, you can define "types" of creatures that share certain attributes. For example, you could say that humans and elves are "good" whereas orcs are "evil":

```
user=> (derive ::human ::good)
user=> (derive ::elf ::good)
user=> (derive ::orc ::evil)
```

You might further say that elves and orcs are "magical" creatures:

```
user=> (derive ::elf ::magical)
user=> (derive ::orc ::magical)
```

Just to make things interesting, let's add a special kind of human, a "hero":

```
user=> (derive ::hero ::human)
```

We have created the graph of relationships shown in Figure 9-1.

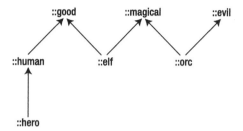

Figure 9-1. *Example hierarchy with arrows pointing from children to parents*

Querying Hierarchies

Once you have defined these relationships, you can query them with the **isa?** function:

```
(isa? child parent)
```

isa? returns true if the child is derived (directly or indirectly) from the parent. For example, the following code:

```
user=> (isa? ::orc ::good)
false
user=> (isa? ::hero ::good)
true
user=> (isa? ::hero ::magical)
false
```

isa? also returns true if the parent and child are the same (as defined by Clojure's = function):

```
user=> (isa? ::human ::human)
true
```

Hierarchies with Multimethods

When a multimethod is searching for the correct method to invoke, it uses the **isa?** function to compare dispatch values. This means that multimethods can dispatch not only on explicit types, but on derived types as well. Here's a multimethod that only works on "magical" creatures:

```
(defmulti cast-spell :species)

(defmethod cast-spell ::magical [creature]
  (str (:name creature) " casts a spell."))
```

```
(defmethod cast-spell :default [creature]
  (str "No, " (:name creature) " is not magical!"))

user=> (cast-spell c)
"Calis casts a spell."
user=> (cast-spell a)
"No, Arthur is not magical!"
```

When the dispatch value is a vector, the multimethod compares each vector element, from left to right, using **isa?**. This combines multiple-argument dispatch with hierarchies. For example, you could redefine your **encounter** multimethod based on "good" and "evil" creatures.

```
(defmulti encounter (fn [x y]
                      [(:species x) (:species y)]))

(defmethod encounter [::good ::good] [x y]
  (str (:name x) " and " (:name y) " say hello."))

(defmethod encounter [::good ::evil] [x y]
  (str (:name x) " is attacked by " (:name y)))

(defmethod encounter [::evil ::good] [x y]
  (str (:name x) " attacks " (:name y)))

(defmethod encounter :default [x y]
  (str (:name x) " and " (:name y)
       " ignore one another."))

user=> (encounter c a)
"Calis and Arthur say hello."
user=> (encounter a d)
"Arthur is attacked by Drung"
```

Hierarchies with Java Classes

Clojure's hierarchies can integrate with and extend Java's class hierarchy. In addition to symbols and keywords, the child argument to derive can also be a Java class. There aren't really any classes in the JDK that fit into your fantasy world, but you could make the (plausible) assertion that the Java Date class is evil:

```
user=> (derive java.util.Date ::evil)
```

The **isa?** function understands both hierarchies and Java class relationships:

```
user=> (isa? java.util.Date ::evil)
true
user=> (isa? Float Number)
true
```

As a result, you can define multimethods that dispatch on **class**, just like Java methods. This example, the **invert** multimethod, is defined to work on both Numbers (by negating them) and Strings (by reversing them):

```
(defmulti invert class)
(defmethod invert Number [x]
  (- x))
(defmethod invert String [x]
  (apply str (reverse x)))
user=> (invert 3.14)
-3.14
user=> (invert "hello")
"olleh"
```

More Hierarchy Queries

Three functions provide additional information about hierarchies.

```
(parents tag)
(ancestors tag)
(descendants tag)
```

All three return sets. **parents** returns the immediate parents of tag, **ancestors** returns all immediate and indirect parents. **descendants** returns all immediate and indirect children of tag.

parents and **ancestors** work on Java classes; **descendants** does not (this is a limitation of the Java type system).

```
user=> (parents ::orc)
#{:user/magical :user/evil}
user=> (descendants ::good)
#{:user/elf :user/hero :user/human}
user=> (parents ::hero)
#{:user/human}
user=> (ancestors ::hero)
#{:user/good :user/human}
user=> (parents java.util.Date)
#{java.lang.Object java.lang.Cloneable
  java.io.Serializable java.lang.Comparable
  :user/evil}
```

Note that the parents of java.util.Date include both the relationships defined by the Java class hierarchy and those you created with **derive**.

Resolving Conflicts

Since Clojure's hierarchies permit multiple inheritance, situations may arise in which there is more than one valid choice for a multimethod. Clojure does not know which one to choose, so it throws an exception.

As an example, consider a multimethod in your fantasy game that has dispatch values for both ::good and ::magical creatures:

```
(defmulti slay :species)

(defmethod slay ::good [creature]
  (str "Oh no!  A good creature was slain!"))

(defmethod slay ::magical [creature]
  (str "A magical creature was slain!"))
```

If you slay a human or an orc, you know what happens:

```
user=> (slay a)  ;; human
"Oh no!  A good creature was slain!"
user=> (slay d)  ;; orc
"A magical creature was slain!"
```

But what happens if you slay an elf?

```
user=> (slay b)
java.lang.IllegalArgumentException:
Multiple methods in multimethod 'slay' match
dispatch value: :user/elf -> :user/magical
and :user/good, and neither is preferred
```

The exception tells us that ::elf is derived from both ::magical and ::good and that there are methods for both.

To deal with this problem, you must specify the order in which dispatch values should be tried. The prefer-method function takes a multimethod and specifies that one dispatch value is preferred over another:

```
(prefer-method multimethod preferred-value other-value)
```

In this example, you would say:

```
user=> (prefer-method slay ::good ::magical)
user=> (slay b)
"Oh no!  A good creature was slain!"
```

The second solution (which isn't really a solution at all) is simply to remove one of the offending methods. The remove-method function takes a multimethod and a dispatch value then deletes the method with that dispatch value.

```
(remove-method multimethod dispatch-value)
```

In this example, it might be:

```
user=> (remove-method slay ::magical)
user=> (slay b)
"Oh no!  A good creature was slain!"
```

Type Tags

The **type** function is a more general version of **class**. First, **type** looks for **:type** metadata (see Chapter 8) on its argument, and returns that. If the object has no **:type** metadata, or if it does not support metadata, **type** returns the object's class:

```
user=> (type (with-meta {:name "Bob"} {:type ::person}))
:user/person
user=> (type 42)
java.lang.Integer
user=> (type {:name "Alice"})
clojure.lang.PersistentArrayMap
```

If you were to redefine your game creatures using **:type** metadata for the species:

```
(def a (with-meta {:name "Arthur", :strength 8}
                  {:type ::human}))
(def b (with-meta {:name "Balfor", :strength 7}
                  {:type ::elf}))
```

You could redefine the **move** multimethod to dispatch on type:

```
(defmulti move type)

(defmethod move ::elf [creature]
  (str (:name creature) " runs swiftly."))

(defmethod move ::human [creature]
  (str (:name creature) " walks steadily."))
```

This would permit the **move** multimethod to work with both metadata-enabled Clojure data structures and ordinary Java objects:

```
(defmethod move Number [n]
  (str "What?! Numbers don't move!"))

user=> (move a)
"Arthur walks steadily."
user=> (move b)
"Balfor runs swiftly."
user=> (move 6.022)
"What?! Numbers don't move!"
```

User-Defined Hierarchies

In addition to the global hierarchy, you can create your own independent hierarchies. The **make-hierarchy** function returns a new hierarchy (essentially a map of parent/child relationships). The **derive**, **isa?**, **parents**, **ancestors**, and **descendants** functions all accept an extra first argument that specifies the hierarchy to use.

Unlike the global hierarchy, user-defined hierarchies allow unqualified (no namespace) keywords or symbols as tags.

Be careful when creating user-defined hierarchies with **derive**, because its behavior is slightly different. When called with two arguments, **derive** modifies the global hierarchy. But user-defined hierarchies are immutable, like Clojure's other data structures, so the three-argument version of **derive** returns the modified hierarchy. This can be seen in the following example:

```
user=> (def h (make-hierarchy))
user=> (derive h :child :parent)
user=> (isa? h :child :parent)
false
```

Therefore, to construct a user-defined hierarchy, you must thread it through the derive statements, as in this example:

```
user=> (def h (-> (make-hierarchy)
                  (derive :one :base)
                  (derive :two :base)
                  (derive :three :two)))
user=> (isa? h :three :base)
true
```

Another alternative is to use one of Clojure's mutable reference types, such as a Var:

```
user=> (def h (make-hierarchy))
user=> (isa? h :child :parent)
false
user=> (alter-var-root (var h) derive :child :parent)
user=> (isa? h :child :parent)
true
```

By default, multimethods use the global hierarchy. The **defmulti** form accepts an optional argument, **:hierarchy**, followed by a different hierarchy to use.

Summary

Multimethods are very flexible, but that flexibility comes at a cost: they are not very efficient. Consider what happens every time you invoke a multimethod: it has to call the dispatch function, look up the dispatch value in a hash table, then perform one or more **isa?** comparisons to find the correct method. Even a smart compiler like Hotspot has trouble optimizing that sequence.

As a result, multimethods are probably not suitable for "low-level" functions that get called very frequently. That's why none of Clojure's built-in functions are multimethods. They are, however, an excellent tool for building extensible "high-level" APIs. Protocols, introduced in Clojure 1.2 and described in Chapter 13, offer a more restricted form of method dispatch with better performance.

CHAPTER 10

Java Interoperability

Calling Java from Clojure

Clojure is built on Java not only because it is a portable, feature-rich platform, but because thousands of libraries, both open-source and commercial, are written in Java. Clojure can leverage all this existing code to get past the "library problem" that plagues most new programming languages.

Clojure does not come packaged with libraries to handle common tasks like file I/O, networking, and database connections. While the number of extant Clojure libraries is growing rapidly, it is still quite small. Fortunately, for any task you might have in mind, there almost certainly exists a Java library to help you with it. The JVM itself comes with over 4000 classes covering everything from networking to GUIs. Clojure is designed to make working with Java libraries as seamless as possible.

Java Interop Special Forms

Clojure uses just three special forms to handle all interactions with Java classes. The **new** special form creates an instance of a class.

```
(new classname & constructor-arguments)
```

new takes the name of a class (a symbol, which will not be evaluated) as its first argument, followed by any arguments for the class's constructor function. The following are some examples:

```
user> (new String)
""
user> (new java.util.Date)
#<Date Thu Oct 29 17:04:19 EDT 2009>
user> (new java.util.Date 55 10 12)
#<Date Sat Nov 12 00:00:00 EST 1955>
```

The . (dot) special form calls Java methods or fields.

```
(. target name & arguments)
```

The **target** argument may be either a class name or an arbitrary expression. If the **target** argument is a class name, then the **name** should be a symbol (which is not evaluated) naming a public *static* method or field of that class. For example, the following code:

```
user=> (. Integer valueOf "42")
42
```

```
user=> (. Integer MAX_VALUE)
2147483647
```

These are equivalent to this Java code:

```
Integer.valueOf(42);
Integer.MAX_VALUE;
```

If **target** is *not* a class name, then it will be evaluated normally, and **name** should be the name of a public *instance* method or field of the resulting object. Here are some examples:

```
user=> (def s "Hello, World!")
#'user/s
user=> (. s substring 0 5)
"Hello"
```

The second expression is equivalent to the Java code:

```
s.substring(0, 5);
```

To set the value of public fields, you can use the **set!** special form like this:

```
(set! (. target name) value)
```

As shown, **target** is an object or symbol naming a class, **name** is a symbol naming a public field of that class or object, and **value** is any expression. This is equivalent to the Java code:

```
target.name = value;
```

The **new**, **.** (dot), and **set!** special forms are just that, *special.* They do not obey the same rules for evaluation as normal Clojure functions and macros. In particular, the **name** argument is never evaluated, so it cannot be determined at run-time. You cannot, for example, do the following:

```
;; bad code!
(defn call-method [object method-name]
  (. object method-name))
```

That will try to call a method named "method-name" on the object—probably not what you wanted. If you need to determine the name of a method at run-time, there are two ways to achieve it: the Java Reflection API and Clojure's **eval** function. The former is preferred, but consult the Reflection API documentation for details.[1]

Java Interop Preferred Forms

While the **new** and **.** (dot) special forms are sufficient for Java interop, some additional syntax helps Java fit better with Clojure's Lisp-based syntax.

First, Java method calls can be made to look more like Clojure function calls by putting the method name at the head of a list, prefixed by a period:

---

[1] `http://java.sun.com/docs/books/tutorial/reflect/`

(*.method object arguments*)

The **.method** form will be processed by the Clojure compiler *as if it were a macro* that expands to:

(**. object method arguments**)

By "as if it were a macro," I mean that this feature is a purely syntactic abstraction or "syntactic sugar." It does not magically transform Java methods into first-class functions.[2] For example, you cannot use **.method** as a function argument to **map**. Instead, you must wrap the method in a Clojure function:

```
user=> (map #(.toUpperCase %) ["one" "two" "three"])
("ONE" "TWO" "THREE")
```

The Clojure macro **memfn** was created for this purpose before the anonymous function syntax **#()** existed. **memfn** takes a symbol and expands to an anonymous function that calls the method named by that symbol. The anonymous function in the preceding example could have been written (**memfn toUpperCase**), but the **#()** form is shorter and preferred.

New instances of Java classes can be constructed by placing the class name at the head of a list, *followed* by a period:

```
user=> (java.util.Date. 110 3 12)
#<Date Mon Apr 12 00:00:00 EDT 2010>
user=> (StringBuilder. "Hello")
#<StringBuilder Hello>
```

You can call static methods with the syntax (**ClassName/method arguments**) and retrieve the value of a static field with **ClassName/field**. For example, the following code:

```
user=> (Integer/parseInt "101")
101
user=> Integer/MIN_VALUE
-2147483648
```

Since these "syntactic sugar" expansions happen in the same compilation phase as macro-expansion, macros that do complex code-generation may need to avoid them and use the **new** and **.** (dot) special forms directly. In all other cases, the "syntactic sugar" forms are preferred.

Clojure Types and Java Interfaces

One of Java's strengths as a platform is the provision of generic interfaces for common datatypes such as lists and sets. Clojure's data structures implement these interfaces where appropriate, so if you need to call a Java method that expects, for example, a java.util.List, you can pass it a Clojure data structure without any conversion. Table 10-1 shows which interfaces are implemented by each of the built-in Clojure types.

---

[2] Method names as first-class functions has been suggested for a future version of Clojure.

Table 10-1.Standard Java Interfaces Implemented by Clojure Types

Java interface	list	vector	map	set	function
java.util.Collection	✓	✓	--	✓	--
java.util.List	✓	✓	--	--	--
java.util.Map	--	--	✓	--	--
java.util.Set	--	--	--	✓	--
java.util.RandomAccess	--	✓	--	--	--
java.lang.Iterable	✓	✓	✓	✓	--
java.lang.Comparable	--	✓	--	--	--
java.lang.Runnable	--	✓	✓	✓	✓
java.util.concurrent.Callable	--	✓	✓	✓	✓
java.util.Comparator	--	--	--	--	✓

Be aware that Clojure's collection types (list, vector, map, and set) are still immutable, so they only implement the read-only portions of the java.util.Collection interfaces. Calling a mutating method (such as `List.add` or `Map.put`) on an immutable object will throw an `UnsupportedOperationException`.

What about Java generics like `List<String>` or `Map<Integer,Object>`? Fortunately, Clojure code never needs to worry about generics due to the way they are implemented in the JVM. Generic types are ignored in Java bytecode; they exist only as hints to the Java language compiler.[3] The Java type `List<String>`, when compiled, is just plain `List`. What this means for Clojure is that you can call a Java method expecting a generic type (e.g., `List<String>`) with an instance of the base collection type (`List`). As long as the collection contains objects of the correct type (`String`), it just works.

Java Arrays

Java arrays lack the concurrency safety of Clojure's collection types; they are mutable and non-thread-safe. However, some Java APIs use arrays for function arguments or return values, so it is necessary to work with them.

---

[3] In contrast, the .NET Common Language Runtime has strongly-typed generics, which are more difficult to implement in a dynamically-typed language like Clojure. This was one reason for the choice of Java as the primary platform for Clojure.

In addition, some algorithms can be implemented more efficiently with primitive arrays, especially algorithms that deal with very large collections of primitive types. Using primitive arrays for performance will be discussed in Chapter 14.

Creating Arrays

You can create a Java array with the make-array function:

```
(make-array type & dimensions)
```

The **type** argument must be a class. If you want an array of a Java primitive type, such as **int** or **double**, you can use the TYPE field of the corresponding class:

```
(make-array Double/TYPE 40)    ;; creates a double[40] array
```

If you give only one dimension to **make-array**, you get a normal Java array of that length. If you give multiple dimensions, you get a multidimensional array, which is implemented in Java as an array of pointers to other arrays.

In addition to **make-array**, there are convenience functions for creating arrays of Java primitive types: **int-array**, **long-array**, **float-array**, and **double-array**. Each can be called in several argument forms:

- **(int-array size)** creates an int[] array of **size** elements.

- **(int-array size initial-value)** does the same and also sets every element to **initial-value**.

- **(int-array collection)** creates an int[] array of the same size as **collection**, filled with the elements of **collection** converted to **int**s.

- **(int-array size collection)** creates an int[] array of **size** elements and fills it with elements from **collection**; any unused array elements will be initialized to zero.

The Clojure function **to-array** takes any Clojure collection type and returns a Java **Object[]** array. If you have a two-dimensional matrix represented as a collection of collections, you can use the **to-array-2d** function to produce a 2-dimensional Java array. For example, the following code:

```
user=> (def matrix [[1 0 0] [0 1 0] [0 0 1]])
#'user/matrix
user=> (to-array-2d matrix)
#<Object[][] [[Ljava.lang.Object;@540984b>
```

If you need to convert a collection into an array of a specific type, you can use the **into-array** function:

```
(into-array collection)
(into-array type collection)
```

Called with one argument, a collection, **into-array** returns an array of the same type as the first item in the collection. Called with two arguments, the first argument is a class specifying the type of the array. For example, the following code:

```
user=> (into-array Comparable ["aa" "bb" "cc"])
#<Comparable[] [Ljava.lang.Comparable;@a00185>
```

Manipulating Arrays

You can retrieve a single value from an array (of any dimensionality) with the **aget** function:

(aget *array* & *indices*)

Setting elements in an array is complicated by the need for special functions for primitive arrays. The **aset** function works on any arrays of any **Object** type:

(aset array index value)
(aset array & indices value)

The setter functions for arrays of primitive types work the same way: **aset-boolean**, **aset-byte**, **aset-char**, **aset-short**, **aset-int**, **aset-long**, **aset-float**, and **aset-double**. Note that these functions are not very efficient; in fact, they are slower than **aset** on type-hinted arrays (see Chapter 14). Use them only when you need to deal with small arrays for Java interop purposes, not for performance.

You can copy an array with the **aclone** function, and get its length with the **alength** function (although **count** also works).

Iterating Over Arrays

The **map** and **reduce** functions will work on Java arrays, but they work by converting the arrays to sequences. For slightly greater efficiency, you can iterate over arrays directly using array-specific macros.

(amap *a idx ret expr*)

The **amap** macro initializes **ret** (a symbol) as a clone of the array **a**, then evaluates **expr** repeatedly with **idx** bound to successive indexes of **a**. Whatever value is returned by **expr**, it will be assigned to the same index of **ret**. Finally, **amap** returns **ret**.

(areduce *a idx ret init expr*)

The **areduce** macro assigns **ret** (a symbol) the value of **init**, then evaluates **expr** repeatedly with **idx** bound to successive indexes of the array **a**. Whatever value is returned by **expr** becomes the new value of **ret**. Finally, **areduce** returns the last value of **ret**.

Note that both **amap** and **areduce** are macros implemented in terms of loop/recur, so they take expressions as arguments instead of the functions used by **map** and **reduce**.

Calling Clojure from Java

Clojure code can generate real Java classes and methods that can be called like any other Java class. However, if you need to call just a few Clojure functions from your Java code, it may be simpler to user Clojure's Java API, which consists of static methods of the classes clojure.lang.RT, clojure.lang.Compiler, and clojure.lang.Var.

Loading and Evaluating Clojure Code

clojure.lang.RT is the Clojure "runtime" class. Remember, Clojure has no interpreter; there cannot be multiple "instances" of Clojure in a single JVM.[4] As a result, most methods of RT are static.

```
class RT {
    ...
    public static void load(String name);
    public static void loadResourceScript(String filename);
    public static void maybeLoadResourceScript(String filename);
    ...
}
```

The **RT.load** method behaves just like the Clojure **load** function described in Chapter 7. The **name** argument is the name of a file on the classpath, minus the ".clj" or ".class" extension.

The **RT.loadResourceScript** method is similar to **load**, except that **filename** must include the ".clj" extension. **RT.maybeLoadResourceScript** is the same, but will not throw an exception if the file does not exist.

```
class RT {
    ...
    public static Object readString(String code);
    ...
}
class Compiler {
    ...
    public static Object eval(Object obj);
    ...
}
```

The **RT.readString** method is equivalent to the Clojure **read-string** function; it takes a string of Clojure source code and returns the data structure represented by that string. The **Compiler.eval** method will evaluate that data structure just like the Clojure **eval** function and return the result.

Using Clojure Functions and Vars

```
class RT {
    ...
    public static Var var(String ns, String name);
    public static Var var(String ns, String name, Object value);
    ...
}
```

The **RT.var** method returns the Clojure Var with the given namespace and name, creating the namespace and interning the Var (see Chapter 7) as needed. The optional third argument sets the initial value, or *root binding*, of the Var.

---

[4] Java Classloaders, however, permit you to create multiple, independent execution contexts within a single JVM. Classloaders are an advanced Java topic outside the scope of this book.

Once you have a Var object, you can retrieve its value with **Var.get**, or call it as a function with **Var.invoke**:

```
class Var {
    ...
    public Object get();
    public Object invoke(Object args...);
    ...
}
```

Creating Java Classes

Often, Clojure's Java API will not be sufficient for integrating Java code with Clojure code. Many Java libraries require you to implement a particular interface or extend a particular base class. Fortunately, Clojure can create real Java classes, with methods that can be called like any other Java method, without requiring you to write any "wrapper" code in Java.

Proxying Java Classes

If you need to implement a Java interface or extend a base class for Java interop purposes, the **proxy** macro should be the first place you look. Each time **proxy** is evaluated, it creates a new instance of a *proxy class*, an anonymous class that inherits from the base class and/or interfaces you specify.

```
(proxy [base-class-and-interfaces...] [constructor-args...]
  (methodName [params...]  method-body...)
  (methodName ...))
```

The first argument to **proxy** is a vector of class and interface names. There may be at most one class (because Java only allows single-class inheritance) and any number of interfaces. If no base class is specified, the proxy class will extend java.lang.Object.

The second argument is a vector of values that should be passed as arguments to the base-class constructor. If the constructor takes no arguments, the vector will be empty, but it must be supplied.

The remaining arguments to proxy are lists of the form **(method [args] body)**, where **method** is the name of a public or protected member of one of the base classes, **args** are the arguments to that method, and **body** is the Clojure code that you want to use to implement the method. In effect, you're defining a Clojure function that will be called by the proxy class whenever the named method is invoked.

Multiple-arity methods (methods that take different numbers of arguments) may be implemented like multiple-arity Clojure functions:

```
(method ([arg] body...) ([arg1 arg2] body...))
```

All of this sounds complicated, but it's really not. Let's look at a real example. The Java SAX classes implement stream-based XML processing with a "push" interface. To use them, you must provide an instance of a class that implements the org.xml.sax.ContentHandler interface. Clojure's own XML libraries use **proxy** for this. Here's a simpler example, a proxy ContentHandler that prints out all the text nodes in the XML document, one per line.

```
(import '(javax.xml.parsers SAXParserFactory)
        '(org.xml.sax ContentHandler)
```

```
         '(org.xml.sax.ext DefaultHandler2)
         '(java.io File))

(defn proxy-handler []
  (proxy [DefaultHandler2]
    []  ;; DefaultHandler2 constructor takes no args
    (characters [ch start length]
       (println (String. ch start length)))))

(defn extract-text [filename]
  (let [parser (.newSAXParser (SAXParserFactory/newInstance))]
    (.parse parser (File. filename) (proxy-handler))))
```

The **proxy-handler** function returns an instance of a proxy for the class
org.xml.sax.ext.DefaultHandler2, which provides no-op implementations of all the
org.xml.sax.ContentHandler methods. The proxy class overrides the **characters** method, which receives
a **char** array, and prints the **String** form of that array. The **extract-text** function creates a new instance
of SAXParser using the SAXParserFactory class, then calls the **parse** method with the input file and the
proxy handler. After loading this code, you can run it like this:

```
user=> (extract-text "path/to/some/file.xml")
```

This will print all the text in the XML file. There will be a lot of blank lines, because your implementation
does not ignore text elements consisting entirely of whitespace.

Proxy methods can access the object on which they were called as the special local variable **this**.
For example, to access the value of a public instance field named **foo** in the current object, a proxy
method could call **(.foo this)**.

It is important to remember that proxies are not true subclasses. Although proxies can override
protected methods, they cannot access private or protected fields of their "parent" class. They cannot
provide their own constructor functions, and they cannot add new methods that are not defined in a
parent class or interface. Proxy instances have generated class names like
clojure.proxy.org.xml.sax.ext.DefaultHandler2.

Proxy methods do not have direct access to the superclass object as with Java's **super** keyword.
However, proxies can call superclass methods with the **proxy-super** macro:

```
(proxy-super method & args)
```

method is a symbol (unevaluated) naming a superclass method, **args** are the arguments to that method.
The corresponding method in the proxied superclass will be invoked on the current object (**this**).

Generating Java Classes

While **proxy** is usually sufficient for dealing with Java APIs, there are occasions when nothing but a real,
concrete Java class will do. You can create such classes in Clojure with the **gen-class** macro, which takes
a series of key-value pairs as arguments:

```
(gen-class
    :name          generated-name
    :extends       base-class-name
    :implements    [interfaces ...]
    :init          initialization-function
```

```
:constructors    {[types ...] [super-types ...], ...}
:post-init       post-initialization-function
:methods         [[name [types ...] return-type], ...]
:main            boolean
:factory         factory-name
:state           state-field-name
:exposes         {field {:get name, :set name}, ...}
:exposes-methods {method exposed, ...}
:prefix          string
:impl-ns         namespace
:load-impl-ns    boolean)
```

No way around it, **gen-class** has a ton of parameters. Fortunately, they're all optional except **:name**, and you rarely need more than a few of them. Before you get into the options, let's look at how **gen-class** works with Java.

When you compile a Java source file with **javac**, you get a Java .class file containing Java bytecode. The bytecode defines the fields and methods of that class and their implementations. When you run **java**, the Java Virtual Machine loads the .class file and executes the bytecode it contains.[5]

Clojure, by contrast, generates bytecode at run time. You can type an expression at the Clojure REPL, or load a .clj file, and Clojure will compile it on-the-fly into Java bytecode, then pass that bytecode to the Java Virtual Machine for execution. This is fine when all your code is in Clojure, but becomes a problem when you want Java code to be able to call Clojure code, because the executable bytecode for Clojure functions doesn't exist until runtime!

Conceivably, you could write a small "wrapper" class in Java, whose methods invoke Clojure functions through Clojure's API, like this:

```java
import clojure.lang.RT;

class MyWrapper {
    public static Object doStuff() {
        return RT.var("my-namespace", "do-stuff").invoke();
    }
}
```

Then, your Java code could call the method **MyWrapper.doStuff()**, which invokes the Clojure function **my-namespace/do-stuff**.

Essentially, **gen-class** does the same thing, without you having to write any Java code. It generates a Java .class file containing "stub" methods that call Clojure functions.

Because **gen-class** needs to generate a .class file, which will presumably be used by other statically-compiled Java classes, it cannot be used at runtime. Instead, it must be invoked in a separate compilation step. Clojure normally compiles code at runtime, so compiling Clojure code *before* it is run is called *ahead-of-time*, or *AOT*, compilation.

Ahead-of-Time Compilation

Any Clojure namespace can be AOT-compiled. There is usually little reason to do so unless **gen-class** is involved. AOT-compiled Clojure code is *not* faster than dynamically-compiled code, and it still requires

---

[5] Early JVMs were implemented as bytecode interpreters. Modern JVM implementations use *just-in-time compilation* to convert the platform-independent Java bytecode into optimized machine code.

the Clojure runtime libraries (clojure.jar). However, AOT-compiled code will start up slightly faster, because the Clojure compiler does not need to compile all the source code when it is loaded, which may be beneficial for large programs.

To compile a namespace, use the **compile** function:

```
(compile name)
```

The **name** argument is a quoted symbol naming the namespace you want to compile. Clojure will load the source file for that namespace, using the same rules as **require** for converting namespace names to file names (see Chapter 7); compile it to Java bytecode and write the bytecode out to .class files in a target directory. One namespace will produce many .class files, one for each function.

The tricky part of AOT-compilation is getting the classpath configured correctly. The target directory where **compile** writes .class files is stored in the Var ***compile-path***. When you call **compile**, both this directory *and* the source .clj file must be available on the Java classpath. The default ***compile-path*** is "classes", assumed to be a directory within the current working directory. You can change it on the Java command line by setting the Java system property "clojure.compile.path".

Here's an example. Suppose you have a project containing three directories: source code in "source", compiled code in "target", and libraries in "lib". Your Clojure code is in the file "source/com/example/my_library.clj", with the following namespace declaration:

```
(ns com.example.my-library)
```

To compile this namespace, you can start Clojure from the root directory of your project like this (all on one line):

```
java -cp lib/clojure.jar:sources:target    ↵
  -Dclojure.compile.path=target  clojure.main
```

Note that the classpath contains three elements: the Clojure JAR file, the "sources" directory, and the "target" directory. (You would add JAR files for any other libraries your project uses.) In addition, the system property clojure.compile.path is set to "target". The "target" directory must exist! Then, at the Clojure REPL, you can run:

```
user=> (compile 'com.example.my-library)
```

This will load the source file from "source/com/example/my_library.clj", compile it, and write a bunch of .class files in the directory "target/com/example/".

Once this is done, you can load and use the namespace **com.example.my-library** *without* the original source files. All you need are the .class files and clojure.jar. Obviously, you shouldn't delete your source files, because you might want to change them and recompile later.

To make it easier to integrate AOT-compilation into build scripts, you can start Java with the class clojure.lang.Compile instead of clojure.main, setting up the classpath and system property as before, passing the namespaces to be compiled as arguments on the command line. In the Apache Ant build system, for example, the XML configuration would contain something like the following snippet:

```
<java classname="clojure.lang.Compile"
      classpath="clojure.jar:target:source">
  <sysproperty key="clojure.compile.path"
               value="target"/>
  <arg value="my.first.namespace"/>
  <arg value="my.second.namespace"/>
</java>
```

How does **gen-class** fit into this? When **compile** is compiling a file that calls **gen-class**, it generates the additional .class files described by the **gen-class** configuration options. At *any other time*, i.e., when not AOT compiling, **gen-class** does nothing.

Basic gen-class Options

Now you're ready to tackle the options to **gen-class**. You will usually only need the first three options, **:name**, **:extends**, and **:implements**, but we cover them all here. Wherever the arguments call for a class or interface name, that name may be given as either a symbol (which will not be evaluated) or a String, and must be fully-qualified with the Java package name.

The **:name** argument is the name of the class to be generated. Remember that this is a Java-style package + class name, so you must use underscores or CamelCase instead of hyphens.

The **:extends** argument is the fully-qualified name of a Java class (not an interface) as either a String or a symbol. The generated class will be a subclass of that class.

The **:implements** argument is a vector of Java interface names. The generated class will be declared to implement those interfaces and will include stub methods for all the methods defined in those interfaces.

Defining Methods for the Generated Class

As explained earlier, the class generated by **gen-class** will only contain stub methods. The implementations of those methods are normal Clojure functions in a namespace. Each Clojure function will have the same name as its corresponding method, with an added prefix. The prefix defaults to "-", and can be changed with the **:prefix** argument to **gen-class**. The functions will be called with the object instance as their first argument. For example, if your generated class implements a Java interface with the methods **doStuff(int i)** and **doMoreStuff(String s)**, your namespace should contain the following function definitions:

```
(defn -doStuff [this i] ...)
(defn -doMoreStuff [this s] ...)
```

By default, **gen-class** uses the current namespace to look up method definitions; this can be changed with the **:impl-ns** argument to **gen-class**.

Adding State to the Generated Class

You may want to create a class that can be called by Java code but preserves Clojure's notions of immutable state. The **:state** argument names a public instance field (of type Object) that will be added to the generated class. Within your methods, you can access the value of this field just like any other Java field. Note that the **:state** field is declared **final**, so it may not be set outside of the object constructor. Typically, the value of the **:state** field will be one of Clojure's mutable reference types (Ref, Agent, or Atom). In this way, you can create stateful Java objects that take advantage of Clojure's transactional semantics.

If your object has **:state**, you must provide a way to initialize it. The **:init** argument names an "initialization function" that is called *before* the superclass constructor, with the same arguments as the constructor. The initialization function must return a vector like **[[args...] state]**, where **state** is the value of the **:state** field and **args** are the arguments that will be passed back to the superclass constructor.

To do additional computation *after* the superclass constructor, the **:post-init** argument names a function that will be called immediately after the superclass constructor(s), with the newly-constructed object as its argument. The **:post-init** function's return value is ignored.

Adding Methods to the Generated Class

By default, the generated class contains stub methods for all non-private methods of the parent class and interfaces. If you want to add to this set of methods, you can do so with the **:methods** option to **gen-class**. Its argument is a vector of method signatures, each of the form **[name [arg-types...] return-type]**. Those methods are then implemented by Clojure functions with prefixed names just like superclass methods. To create a static method, add **:static true** metadata to the signature vector.

For example, suppose you want to add two methods to your class with the following Java signatures:

```
public int add(int a, int b);
public static String getNextID();
```

You would use **gen-class** like this:

```
(gen-class ...
  :methods [[add [int int] int]
            #^{:static true} [getNextID [] String]])
...
(defn -add [this a b] ...)
(defn -getNextID [] ...)
```

Remember that **:methods** is only used for adding methods that *do not exist* in the superclass/superinterfaces. You do not need to redefine the signatures of existing Java methods.

Adding Constructors and Factories

The generated class will automatically have public constructors with type signatures matching those of the superclass constructors. You can add additional constructors with the **:constructors** option to **gen-class**. The argument to **:constructors** is a map of the form **{[types...] [super-types...], ...}**. The keys of the map are vectors of argument types for the added constructors, which must map to an existing superclass constructor, identified by a vector of its argument types. For example, if your generated class **:extends** a class **Foo** with a constructor **Foo(int, int)**, and you want to add a constructor that takes a single **String** argument, you can do so with the following gen-class form:

```
(gen-class ...
  :constructors {[String] [int int]} ...)
```

You must also supply an **:init** function that accepts and returns the appropriate types.

Some Java development styles encourage static factory methods instead of public constructors. You can add static factory methods to your generated class with the **:factory** option to **gen-class**. Its argument is the name of the generated factory method; this method will be overloaded to accept all the same argument types as the constructors.

Exposing Superclass Members

Because your method implementations are Clojure functions, not true Java methods, they do not have access to protected fields of the superclass, nor can they call superclass methods. To work around this, you can add the `:exposes` and `:exposes-methods` options to `gen-class`.

`:exposes` takes a map of the form `{field {:get getter, :set setter}, ...}`. Each key is the name of a protected instance field of the superclass, the value specifies the names of public getter and setter methods that will be added to the generated class. You do not need to provide implementations for these methods; they are generated automatically.

`:exposes-methods` takes a map of the form `{super exposed, ...}`, where `super` is the name of a superclass method, and `exposed` is the name of a public method that will be added to the generated class. The exposed method calls the super method. You can use this feature when, for example, your implementation of a method needs to call the superclass version of the same method.

Generating Command-Line Programs

Java allows any class to be run as command-line executable, provided it has a method declared `public static void main(String[] args)`. You can specify `:main true` in `gen-class` to add the static main method to your generated class. The function implementing this method should be called `-main` (unless you changed the prefix). Rather than a single array argument, it will be called with however many arguments are present on the command line. An easy way to handle this is to define the function to take a variable number of arguments:

```
(gen-class ...
  :main true ...)
(defn -main [& args] ...)
```

Once you have compiled a namespace with a `:main` method, you can execute it at the command line like this:

```
java -cp ...  your.class.name  arguments...
```

Remember that your compiled .class files and the Clojure JAR must be on the classpath.

Loading the Implementation

By default, any class generated with `gen-class` will automatically load its implementing namespace from the classpath the first time it is used, just as if you had `require`'d the namespace. If you are using some alternative code loading mechanism and you do not want the generated class to interfere, add the `:load-impl-ns false` option to `gen-class`.

Namespace Declarations with gen-class

`gen-class` can appear as part of a namespace declaration in the `ns` macro. In this case, it is written as `(:gen-class options...)`. Within `ns`, the `:name` and `:impl-ns` options default to the namespace being declared and `:main` defaults to `true`. Everything else is the same. However, remember that you need not limit yourself to one namespace per generated class. You could generate several classes, with different `:prefix` options, and put all the method implementations in the same Clojure namespace.

Simple Command-Line Program

If all you need is a program that can be run at the command line, you only need a **-main** function and an **ns** declaration containing **(:gen-class)**, as in this example:

```
(ns com.example.app
  (:gen-class))

(defn -main [& args]
  (println "Hello, World!"))
```

When AOT-compiled into a directory named *classes*, this example can be run with the command:

```
java -cp classes:clojure.jar com.example.app
```

Summary

Clojure is not intended to replace the Java language. Rather, it is designed to augment the capabilities of the Java platform with a different style of programming. Newcomers to Clojure may dislike the intrusion of Java class and method names into their Clojure code, and rush to wrap every Java method call in a Clojure function. More experienced Clojure programmers appreciate the power offered by Java libraries and are comfortable mixing Java methods and Clojure functions. The world is too big to implement everything from scratch. Clojure takes advantage of the vast ecosystem of Java libraries and lives comfortably in a Java-based environment.

CHAPTER 11

■■■

Parallel Programming

Parallelism in Clojure

Chapter 6 spends a lot of time discussing how Clojure manages state safely in a concurrent environment. State management is definitely the trickiest part of concurrent programming, and the attention Clojure pays to getting state management right is well spent.

However, discussions of state management do not address how a program becomes parallel to begin with, and the best strategies for splitting the execution of a program among various threads. Although it's not as sticky a problem, it's still important to understand. Knowing how and when to distribute execution among multiple threads will allow you to maximize concurrency in your program, making it faster and guaranteeing scalability as it is run on machines with more and more processors.

Clojure offers a variety of techniques for introducing concurrency, ranging in levels of abstraction from high-level concepts such as agents all the way down to JVM primitives, accessible through the Java interoperability features. Some techniques are more suitable for data-centric concurrency while others for a more hands-on approach to threading.

This chapter will outline the various ways you can introduce concurrency into a Clojure program and the pros and cons of each.

Agents

Agents are discussed in Chapter 6, although primarily in their aspect as identities used for managing state. Agents are interesting because they bridge the gap between managing state and managing execution: they do both. Again, review Chapter 6 for a detailed discussion on how to create and send actions to agents. This section deals primarily with their concurrency characteristics and implications.

Agent Thread Pools

In their execution aspect, agents are run in thread pools managed by the Clojure runtime. Actions sent to agents will be queued and then executed in one of two thread pools, depending on whether the action was dispatched using the send or send-off function.

The thread pool used by the send function is sized and tuned to match the number of physical processors available to the JVM. This optimizes throughput for CPU-intensive actions: the number of actions executing concurrently will be roughly equal to the number of physical CPUs. If an action is dispatched while all threads in the thread pool (and, therefore, CPUs) are busy, it is queued and will execute in turn.

The thread pool used by the send-off function is *not* limited to the number of physical processes available, but can contain an arbitrarily larger number of processes. The reasoning behind this is that high-latency tasks such as accessing a remote resource will spend most of their time waiting. As such, it's more efficient to allow many processes to time-share on the same processor.

If you send where send-off would be appropriate, or vice-versa, it's not the end of the world. Your program will still be correct: the action will still execute, it just won't be as efficient as possible. If a high-latency action is dispatched with send, it will utilize one of the send-threads until the action completes without actually doing much work. If a CPU-intensive action is dispatched with send-off, it could be pre-empted by the operating system thread scheduler much more often than it would otherwise be, but will still eventually complete.

Agent Example

For an example of a processing-intensive agent, say you had an agent that maintained an average of a list of numbers. The value of the agent could be a map with two keys: the list of numbers, and the current average.

```
user=> (def my-average (agent {:nums [] :avg 0}))
#'user/my-average
```

Now, let's define a function which you'll use as the action function for the agent. It takes two arguments: the current value of an agent, and the number to add, and returns a new agent value.

```
(defn update-average [current n]
    (let [new-nums (conj (:nums current) n)]
        {:nums new-nums
         :avg (/ (reduce + new-nums) (count new-nums))}))
```

In this case, because the action is straightforward processing, with no IO, you'll definitely want to use send and not send-off. Let's send it a few values and see what happens.

```
user=> (send my-average update-average 10)
#<Agent @4cdac8 {:nums [], :avg 0}>

user=> (send my-average update-average 20)
#<Agent @4cdac8 {:nums [10], :avg 10}>

user=> (send my-average update-average 10)
#<Agent @4cdac8 {:nums [10 20], :avg 15}>

user=> (send my-average update-average 20)
#<Agent @4cdac8 {:nums [10 20 10], :avg 40/3}>
```

Finally, let's check the result:

```
user=> @my-average
{:nums [10 20 10 20], :avg 15}
```

It seems to work. However, because you used send, and because the update-average involves just processing and waiting for IO, you can be sure that the agent processes its sends at full speed.

Concurrent Agent Performance

Agents scale very well with the number of CPUs in a machine. If an algorithm or process consists of discrete "tasks" (or if it can be broken down that way), agents are an excellent choice. There are anecdotes of agent-based programs scaling nearly linearly to systems with hundreds of CPUs without any code modification. Of course, your mileage will vary based on exactly what the agents are doing.

Concurrency Functions

There are certain functions and macros in the Clojure standard library which initiate parallel processing. They are extremely convenient, because they require no work to set up and are often a drop-in replacement for their serial counterparts.

There are three built-in concurrent tools: pmap, pvalues, and pcalls. They provide similar functionality: in fact, under the hood, the other two are defined in terms of pmap. From this simple basis, it is possible to build a wide array of very useful concurrency tools.

To provide meaningful examples of concurrency, it is necessary to use a function that takes a non-trivial amount of time to execute. It's rarely worth it to parallelize a task which takes only a few processor instructions. To do this, you can create a function which takes another function as an argument, and returns a "heavy" version of it—a version which waits for one second then returns. This transformation function is defined as follows:

```
(defn make-heavy [f]
    (fn [& args]
        (Thread/sleep 1000)
        (apply f args)))
```

You can verify that this works by using it instead of a normal function and using the built-in time macro to time how long an expression takes to evaluate. For example, a normal call to + takes almost no time at all:

```
user=> (time (+ 5 5))
"Elapsed time: 2.0E-6 msecs"
10
```

As expected, wrapping the + function in make-heavy takes just about a second.

```
user=> (time ((make-heavy +) 5 5))
"Elapsed time: 1001.128155 msecs"
10
```

You will use this technique to observe what kind of advantages using parallel functions can actually give.

pmap

pmaps' signature and functionality are identical to the normal map function. The only difference is that the supplied function is applied to the supplied sequence in parallel, utilizing a number of threads corresponding to the number of CPUs on the system.

pmap is partially lazy in that the entire result set is not realized unless required, but the parallel computation does run ahead of the consumption to some degree.

An example follows, demonstrating similarity to map:

```
user=> (pmap inc [1 2 3 4])
(2 3 4 5)
```

To see how this introduces parallelism, let's use the heavy function, and first see how long it takes using the standard version of map. You'll also use the doall function to force evaluation of the entire value.

```
user=> (time (doall (map (make-heavy inc) [1 2 3 4 5])))
"Elapsed time: 5002.96291 msecs"
(2 3 4 5 6)
```

This shows that the normal map runs the heavy version of the inc function five times. Since it's in the same thread, and each function call takes a full second, this adds up to just about five seconds.

Now, using pmap instead of map:

```
user=> (time (doall (pmap (make-heavy inc) [1 2 3 4 5])))
"Elapsed time: 1031.941815 msecs"
(2 3 4 5 6)
```

It takes only about a second, because although it is still calling the heavy version of inc five times, the calls are happening in parallel. The extra 30 milliseconds observed are the extra time required to set up the additional threads.

pvalues

pvalues takes any number of expressions and returns a lazy sequence of the values of each expression, evaluated in parallel.

```
user=> (pvalues (+ 5 5) (- 5 3) (* 2 4))
(10 2 8)
```

pcalls

pcalls takes any number of no-argument functions and returns a lazy sequence of their return values, executing them in parallel.

```
user=> (pcalls #(+ 5 2) #(* 2 5))
(7 10)
```

Overhead and Performance

For computationally expensive operations, these concurrency functions can provide huge speedups for almost no effort. However, for less expensive computations, they may not be appropriate.

When concurrency functions run, they break the arguments into units of work and dispatch them for execution. This process carries its own computational load, and if the actual computations specified are faster than the overhead involved in setting up their execution, the net result will be *slower* than the non-parallel version.

This means that whether using a concurrency function is beneficial depends on the "weight" of the execution involved. If it's lightweight, such as a basic math operation (as in the preceding examples), don't bother. The cost of setting up the parallel execution exceeds the benefit. If it's very heavyweight, with each computation performing a significant amount of work, parallelizing is a no-brainer and will almost always provide great gains. For the middle ground, experimentation is sometimes necessary to determine whether using the parallel version of a function is worthwhile. You can try increasing the size of each parallel execution, for example, by grouping multiple items together and distributing the processing across the groups, rather than across each item.

To demonstrate, compare the time required to use pmap as opposed to map on a lightweight operation: for example, the normal, light version of inc.

```
user=> (time (dorun (map inc (range 1 1000))))
"Elapsed time: 9.150946 msecs"
```

```
user=> (time (dorun (pmap inc (range 1 1000))))
"Elapsed time: 182.349073 msecs"
```

This shows clearly how the extra cost of assigning threads and farming out work cost vastly more than the benefits of performing the work in parallel.

Futures and Promises

Futures and promises are two slightly more low-level threading constructs, inspired by the similar features available in the Java 6 concurrency API. They are simple to understand, simple to use, and provide a very direct way to spawn threads using native Clojure syntax.

Futures

A Clojure future represents a computation, running in a single thread. As soon as the future is created, a new thread is created and starts executing the computation. When the computation finishes, the thread is recycled and the resulting value can be retrieved from the future by dereferencing it. Alternatively, if the computation is not yet finished when the future is dereferenced, the dereferencing thread will block until the computation is complete.

To create a future, use the future macro, which takes any number of expressions, and yields a future which will evaluate all the expressions and return the last value. For example, the following code:

```
user=> (def my-future (future (* 100 100)))
#'user/my-future
user=> @my-future
10000
```

In this example, the actual value of (* 100 100) is calculated in a separate thread. In a real program, such a trivial expression probably wouldn't be worth putting in a future. To create a simulation of a long-running process, use Java's Thread.sleep() method, which can be invoked from Clojure by Thread/sleep. It pauses execution of the current thread for the specified number of milliseconds.

```
user=> (def my-future (future (Thread/sleep 10000)))
'#user/my-future
```

This future will take ten seconds to complete. If you enter the following at the REPL within ten seconds of the previous statement, you can witness how dereferencing a future blocks the dereferencing thread if it isn't yet complete.

```
user=> @my-future
nil
```

The system will pause visibly for the remainder of the ten seconds of the future's execution before returning the future's result. In this case, `nil`.

You can also create a future using the `future-call` function. It works similarly to the `future` macro, only instead of taking expressions as parameters, it takes a single no-argument function and calls the function in a separate thread while returning a future. You can dereference and inspect the future in exactly the same way as futures created by the basic `future` macro.

Controlling Futures

Clojure includes several functions that can be used to inspect and control futures.

future-cancel

It is possible to attempt to cancel a future that hasn't yet finished executing. This only works under certain circumstances, because the cancellation uses Java's thread interruption mechanism. In order for a computation to be canceled, it needs to internally check the thread's interruption status from time to time or call a method that does (for example, `Thread/sleep`). For details on how to do this, see the Java threading documentation.

`future-cancel` takes a single argument, the future itself. If the future is already complete, cancelling has no effect. If a future has been cancelled before it completed, attempting to dereference the future will cause a `CancellationException` error.

future-cancelled?

future-cancelled? takes a single future as an argument and returns `true` if it has been cancelled. It may be used to check if a call to `future-cancel` succeeded, and therefore if a future is safe to dereference or not.

future-done?

future-done? takes a single future as an argument and returns `true` if the future's execution is complete, otherwise `false`. This function is useful for determining if dereferencing a future will cause blocking or not.

future?

future? takes a single value as an argument and returns `true` if it is a future, otherwise false.

Promises

A promise is a value that may not yet exist. If a promise is dereferenced before its value is set, the dereferencing thread blocks until a value is delivered to the promise. Unlike the other features described in this chapter, promises do not actually cause concurrent execution, but they are often useful to manage execution flow (particularly in concert with futures) and so they are covered here.

When a promise's value is set, all threads waiting for a promise get the value and are released. Any dereferences of the promise after its value is delivered.

To create a promise, simply call the promise function with no arguments.

```
user=> (def my-promise (promise))
'#user/my-promise
```

To deliver a value to a promise, use the deliver function, which takes two arguments, a promise and a value, and returns the promise. The deliver function may only be called once per promise: it throws an exception if called a second time on for the same promise.

```
user=> (deliver my-promise 5)
#<AFn$IDeref&db53459f@1465272: 5>
```

The promise can then be dereferenced as follows:

```
user=> @my-promise
5
```

■ **Caution** Be careful! It is entirely possible to throw your program into a deadlock with promises. Make sure that promises eventually do get a value delivered to them, otherwise, they will block forever. In the preceding example, if you were to dereference my-promise at the REPL before you call deliver, the REPL thread would block, preventing you from ever giving the promise a value. You'd be forced to restart the whole program.

Promises have limited usefulness within a Clojure program: usually, it's better to use a higher level concurrency construct. But for scenarios where it's desirable to manually cause threads to wait, or to hand off execution between threads, promises provide an easy mechanism for doing so.

Java-based Threading

If none of Clojure's other concurrency tools meet your needs for any reason, there's always the option of falling back to Java's native threading capabilities. Through Clojure's Java interoperability features, these work just as well as they do in Java. In some ways, they're even easier to use due to the fact that all Clojure functions implement the java.lang.Runnable interface, so they can be passed directly to threads. Also, Clojure's macros can be used to eliminate a lot of Java's boilerplate code.

A complete discussion of Java concurrency is beyond the scope of this chapter (or this book). However, this section will demonstrate a common task: creating a single thread. The same methods can be applied to the rest of Java's concurrency API. For information and a tutorial on Java's concurrency API, see http://java.sun.com/docs/books/tutorial/essential/concurrency/.

Creating a Thread

The most basic way to create a thread in Java is by instantiating a new java.lang.Thread object, passing it a runnable in its constructor, and calling its start() method. The same can be accomplished in Clojure. The following code demonstrates:

```
user=> (def value (atom 0))
#'user/value
```

First, you create an atom that stores a value. This isn't actually part of the thread code, but you need some way to obtain evidence that the thread actually ran, and you can do that by updating the value of an atom.

```
user=> (def my-thread (Thread. #(swap! value inc)))
#'user/my-thread
```

This creates a thread object by invoking the java.lang.Thread constructor, which takes a single runnable as its argument. In this case, you provide a simple inline function—all functions are runnables in Clojure. Then, to start the thread, simply call the start() method:

```
user=> (.start my-thread)
nil
```

And, to verify that the thread actually ran:

```
user=> @value
1
```

It's worth mentioning that this is far from the *best* way to create a thread in Java. Usually, you'll want to use the executor framework, explained in the previous URL link. However, the same techniques of creating threads and passing them Clojure functions as Runnables apply.

Summary

Clojure has a variety of mechanisms for introducing concurrency, and they follow a rough hierarchy of abstraction:

- The lowest level concurrency feature set in Clojure is Java's built-in concurrency library. It can do everything Java can, but lacks the ease of use of some of Clojure's more advanced features.

    - For very simple control of spawning threads, use Clojure's Futures. If you need to force threads to wait for each other in a certain pattern, you can force threads to block using Promises.

    - For executing the same action on multiple pieces of data in parallel, it's hard to beat Clojure's parallel functions. If an algorithm uses the map function, then it can often be made parallel simply by replacing map with pmap.

- For a high-level, pool-based thread management system that handles both state and execution, use Clojure's Agents.

Successfully writing a highly parallel Clojure program consists of choosing the correct threading model, using the methods previously listed, and managing state safely (as described in Chapter 10). Clojure provides the tools, making it as easy as possible to do both.

■ ■ ■

CHAPTER 12

Macros and Metaprogramming

What Is Metaprogramming?

Metaprogramming is the use of code to modify or create other code. It is primarily a developer tool and acts as a force multiplier, allowing large amounts of predictable code to be generated from just a few statements in the host language (or "metalanguage"). It is extremely useful for automating repetitive, boilerplate code.

Most programming languages support some form of metaprogramming. C has a preprocessor and C++ has templates. Java has annotations and aspect-oriented programming extensions. Scripting languages have "eval" statements. Most languages have some sort of API that can be used to introspect or modify the core language features (such as classes and methods). As a last resort, any language can be used to build source code using string manipulation and then feed it to a compiler.

Code vs. Data

Whatever the implementation, metaprogramming systems have one feature in common: they manipulate code as data. Conceptually, programs *execute* code and *consume* or *produce* data as input and output. By definition, metaprogramming inverts this relationship. Programs *consume* or *produce* code (as their data), so when the generated program runs, it is *executing* data (as its code).

For most languages, treating code as data or data as code is a more or less a cumbersome process, depending on the type of data which represents the code.

One common strategy is to treat code as a textual string. Code can be created by concatenating keywords, variable names, and textual symbols, witht4 the resulting text fed back to the languages parser or evaluator. Needless to say, this can be quite messy and confusing for all but the simplest metaprogramming tasks.

Another strategy is to provide a set of APIs that expose the *concepts* of a programming language as objects within the language, allowing the programmer to make calls such as **createClass()** or **addMethod()**, to build code structures programmatically. This is much more effective than writing and parsing strings, and is used extensively in many object-oriented languages. In this case, the *data* is objects, which have a special relationship with the language runtime.

Homoiconicity

Clojure (and other Lisps) provide a third way of handling the code/data distinction: there is no distinction. In Clojure, all code is data and all data is code.

This property is called *homoiconicity*, which means that the language's code is represented in terms of the language's data structures. For example, this is a line of code in Clojure:

```
(println "Hello, world")
```

167

And this is a sequence (data):

```
'(println "Hello, world")
```

There is only one slight difference—the leading single quote. This is simply an instruction to Clojure that itshould only read the list, instead of reading it and immediately evaluating it, as it would in the first snippet. Forms like this (called *quoted* forms) stop after reading, rather than going on to be evaluated.

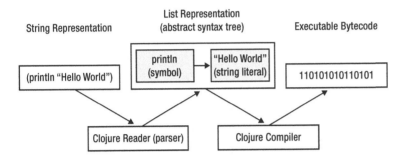

Figure 12-1. *How Clojure code is loaded*

The key point is that Clojure source code isn't fundamentally comprised of strings: Clojure source code is comprised of data structure literals—vectors, maps, and sequences of symbols, literals, and other sequences. In Clojure, data structures are very, very easy to work with, thanks to the sequence abstraction. Metaprogramming is no more difficult than creating a list.

Macros

Macros are the primary means of metaprogramming in Clojure. A Clojure macro is a construct which can be used to transform or replace code before it is compiled. Syntactically, they look a lot like functions, but with several crucial distinctions:

- Macros shouldn't return values directly, but a form.

- Arguments to macros are passed in without being evaluated. They can then be altered, ignored, or added to the macro's output.

- Macros are evaluated only at compile-time.

When you use a macro in your code, what you are really telling Clojure to do is to replace your macro expression with the expression returned by the macro. This is a powerful means of abstraction, and is very useful for implementing control structures or eliminating boilerplate or "wrapper" code.

For example, it is possible to define a macro called **triple-do** which takes one expression as an argument, and replaced it with a **do** form which evaluates the expression three times. The programmer would only type the following expression:

```
(triple-do (println "Hello"))
```

However, this would actually be compiled as *this* expression:

```
(do (println "Hello") (println "Hello") (println "Hello"))
```

Aside from debugging it, there's no need for the programmer ever to need to see or worry about this intermediate form. They can use it directly in their programs, and not worry about the complexity tucked underneath:

```
user=> (triple-do (println "Hello"))
Hello
Hello
Hello
nil
```

Working with Macros

To create a macro, use the **defmacro** macro. This defines a function and registers it as a macro with the Clojure compiler. From then on, when the compiler encounters the macro, it will call the function and use the return value instead of the original expression.

defmacro takes basically the same arguments as **defn**: a name, an optional documentation string, a vector of arguments, and a body. As previously mentioned, the body should evaluate to a valid Clojure form. If the form returned by the macro function is syntactically invalid, it will cause an error wherever it is used.

For example, the following code defines the very simple **triple-do** macro already mentioned:

```
(defmacro triple-do [form]
    (list 'do form form form))
```

This simply uses the built-in **list** function to create a list of four items: the **do** special form and three repetitions of the provided form. Note that **do** is quoted, so it is added to the resultant list as a symbol, rather than being evaluated in place in the body of the macro. If the provided form is **(println "test")**, this list will be **(do (println "test") (println "test") (println "test"))**. This list is valid Clojure syntax, and so the macro works:

```
user=> (triple-do (println "test"))
test
test
test
nil
```

As another example of the possibilities of macros, it is possible write a macro that rewrites an infixed mathematical expression as a standard Clojure prefixed expression, so it can be evaluated. For example, it might transform **(1 + 1)** to the more standard (in Clojure) **(+ 1 1)**. Prefix notation is the Lisp standard and is preferable for all programming tasks. Don't use something like this in your main Clojure code. However, this type of functionality could be useful for writing Domain Specific Languages (DSLs) for people who didn't know Lisp.

When developing, it's first helpful to have a clear idea of what you want the input and output expression to be. For this macro, you want to convert expressions like:

```
(infix (2 + 3))
```

to:

```
(+ 2 3)
```

The macro definition is:

```
(defmacro infix [form]
  (cons (second form) (cons (first form) (nnext form))))
```

It introspects the provided form, and uses **cons** to build a new expression, starting with the second item (the operator), then the first item (the first number), then any additional items. You can verify that it works using the following code:

```
user=> (infix (2 + 3))
5
```

Again, in general, it's bad form to go around redefining the standard way forms are evaluated. Typically, users should get consistent behavior whether their expression is within a macro or not. Still, this example demonstrates the power of macros, and occasionally there are good reasons to do such drastic transformations on expressions.

Debugging Macros

Using macros can be somewhat mind-bending, since you have to keep in mind not only the code you're writing, but the code you're generating. Clojure provides two functions that help debug macros as you write them: **macroexpand** and **macroexpand-1**. They both take a single quoted form as an argument. If the form is a macro expression, they return the expanded result of the macro without evaluating it, making it possible to inspect and see exactly what a macro is doing. **macroexpand** expands the given form repeatedly until it is no longer a macro expression. **macroexpand-1** expands the expression only once. Both of them expand only the macro forms present in the original expression; they don't recursively expand additional macros present in the output.

The following example shows **macroexpand** applied to the macros defined in the previous section:

```
user=> (macroexpand '(triple-do (println "test")))
 (do (println "test") (println "test") (println "test")))

user=> (macroexpand '(infix (2 + 3)))
 (+ 2 3)
```

You can use different expressions with **macroexpand**, to see what the output for any arguments to your macro looks like, even though it can quickly become complicated:

```
user=> (macroexpand '(triple-do (do (println "a") (println "b"))))
 (do (do (println "a") (println "b")) (do (println "a") (println "b")) (do (println "a")
(println "b")))
```

Sometimes, you can see errors before they occur. For example, if you pass an expression to the **infix** macro that is already prefixed, it will actually reverse the process and *infix* the result, which is:

```
user=> (macroexpand '(infix (+ 1 2)))
 (1 + 2)
```

Using **macroexpand** gives an opportunity to see potential problems before you actually try evaluating them. You can also run unit tests against the output of **macroexpand** to verify that your macros are behaving as expected.

Code Templating

Manually creating forms to return from macro functions can sometimes be tedious. Worse, with complex macros it can be difficult to determine what the output form will actually be.

To alleviate this problem, Clojure provides a code templating system. Effectively, it allows macro developers to enter the return forms of macros as literals, splicing in values where necessary.

The templating system is based around the syntax-quote character, a backquote: `. Syntax quoting works almost exactly the same as regular quoting with single-quote, with one major exception: you can use the unquote symbol (the tilde, ~) to insert a value at any point within the syntax-quoted expression. Also, symbols directly referenced within a syntax quote are assumed to be top level, namespace-qualified symbols and will be expanded as such.

For example, take the macro body of **triple-do**. It explicitly uses the **list** function to construct a list for return. Of course, the easier way to represent a list in code is to enter it as a literal, using the single quote. However, it's then impossible to modify it. By using syntax-quote, and by using unquote within it to insert values, it *is* possible.

The templated version of the **triple-do** macro looks like the following:

```
(defmacro template-triple-do [form]
    `(do ~form ~form ~form))
```

The **do** expression is represented as a list literal, and the return value of the macro function. It uses the syntax-quote character to ensure that it is treated as a literal and not evaluated right away. *Inside* the syntax-quote are three unquotes; they actually insert the value of the **form** parameter at that point inside the literal value.

The expansion of **template-triple-do** is identical to the original version:

```
user=> (macroexpand '(template-triple-do (println "test")))
 (do (println "test") (println "test") (println "test"))
```

Splicing Unquotes

Unquoting sequences within a syntax-quote doesn't always work out quite as intended. Sometimes, it is desirable to insert the *contents* of a sequence the templated list, rather than the list itself. To see why, try implementing the **infix** macro described previously, using templating:

```
(defmacro template-infix [form]
    `(~(second form) ~(first form) ~(nnext form)))
```

It looks like it should work fine. But try expanding it:

```
user=> (macroexpand '(template-infix (1 + 3)))
 (+ 1 (3))
```

There's an extra set of parenthesis around the 3, which will cause problems. The reason is that the **~(nnext form)** expression resolves to a list, not an individual symbol. In this case, you want to insert the *contents* of the sequence returned by **(nnext form)**, not the sequence itself.

To insert the contents of a list, use the *splicing unquote*, denoted by ~@. ~@ inserts the *values* of a sequence consecutively into a parent sequence. Using it instead of the normal unquote in the **template-infix** macro yields the correct results:

```
(defmacro template-infix [form]
    `(~(second form) ~(first form) ~@(nnext form)))

user=> (macroexpand '(template-infix (1 + 3)))
 (+ 1 3)
```

Generating Symbols

One very important rule of Clojure macros is that while it is possible to create and bind local symbols in macro-generated code, the names of such locals may *not* conflict with any existing symbols. But this is problematic: when writing a macro, it is impossible to know all of the potential contexts in which a macro might later be run. So Clojure enforces the rule: don't bind named symbols in macros.

Still, sometimes it's necessary to define local symbols in a macro. To get around this restriction, Clojure provides a feature called *auto gensym* within syntax quoted forms. Within any syntax-quoted form (forms using the back-tick, `), you can append the # character to the end of any local symbol name, and when the macro is expanded, it will replace the symbol with a randomly generated symbol that is guaranteed not to conflict with anything, and which will match any other symbol created with auto gensym in the same syntax-quote template. As long as you use the auto gensym feature on them, you can define as many local symbols as you like within your macros.

To see an example of this, consider a macro called **debug-println** which performs the same function as **println**, but instead of returning nil, it returns the value of the expression. This allows it to be used inside expressions and debug them. You want to be able to use it like this:

```
(+ 5 (* 4 (debug-println (/ 4 3))))
```

First, determine what you want the generated code to look like. In this case, it's as follows:

```
(let [result (/ 4 3)]
    (println (str "Value is: " result))
    result)
```

Then build the macro definition. Note how the **result** symbol is using the auto gensym feature:

```
(defmacro debug-println [expr]
    `(let [result# ~expr]
        (println (str "Value is: " result#))
        result#))
```

Calling **macroexpand-1** shows the generated symbol name:

```
user=> (macroexpand '(debug-println (/ 4 3)))
(clojure.core/let [result_2349_auto (/ 4 3)]
    (clojure.core/println (clojure.core/str "Value is: " result_2349_auto)
    result_2349_auto)
```

With the exception of the alternate name for the result symbol, and the fully qualified function names, it looks exactly like what we originally wanted. And it works!

```
user=> (+ 5 (* 4 (debug-println (/ 4 3))))
Value is: 4/3
31/3
```

When to Use Macros

Macros are extremely powerful and allow you to control and abstract code in ways that would not be otherwise possible. However, using them does come at a cost. They operate at a higher level of abstraction, and so they are significantly more difficult to reason about then normal code. If a problem occurs, it can be much trickier to debug, since there's an extra level of indirection between where the problem actually is, and where the error message originates.

Therefore, the best way to use macros is to use them as little as possible. A few macros go a long way. Most things you need macros for (including some of the examples in this chapter) could also be accomplished with first-class functions. When you can, do that instead, and *don't* use macros.

That said, there are certain situations where using a macro is the best, easiest, or the only way to accomplish a given task. Usually, they fall into one of the following categories:

- *Implement control structures*: One of the main differences between macros and functions is that the arguments of macros are not evaluated. If you need to write a control structure that might not evaluate some of its parameters, it has to be a macro.

- *Wrap* **def** *or* **defn:** Usually, you only want to call **def** or **defn** at compile time. Calling them programmatically while a program is running is usually a recipe for disaster. So, if you need to wrap their behavior in additional logic, the best place to do it is usually a macro.

- *Performance*: Because they are expanded at compile time, using a macro can be faster than calling a function. Usually, this doesn't make much of a difference, but in extremely tight loops, you can sometimes eke out performance by eliminating a function call or two and using macros instead.

- *Codify reoccurring patterns:* Macros can be used to formalize any commonly occurring pattern in your code. In essence, macros are your means of modifying the language itself to suit your needs. Macros aren't the *only* way to do this, but they can sometimes do it in a way that is least invasive to other parts of your code.

Using Macros

Understanding macros and knowing when to use them can be a daunting proposition, so it is helpful to look at a range of examples to gain a sense of what macros can be used for. Unfortunately, no selection of examples can entirely cover the types of things you can do with macros: macros represent no less than an ability to change the language itself, and the potential ways one might want to do so are limitless. However, there are some common patterns that are often implemented with macros and being familiar with them can give you a head start in understanding when they can be useful.

Implementing a Control Structure

As mentioned, one of the important distinctions between macros and functions is that since macros are expanded before compilation, rather than at runtime, it is possible that their arguments might not be evaluated at all. This is an essential component of control structures, where it is necessary that only *some* of the provided expressions actually evaluate, not all of them.

Consider a control form which takes two expressions and executes only one of them randomly. This might be used in a game, or in an artificial intelligence implementation. You want it to look something like the following:

```
(rand-expr (println "A") (println "B") )
```

This cannot be implemented as a function, since both **println** statements are evaluated as arguments before **rand-expr** is even called. But you want only *one* of the expressions to evaluate at random. This can only be accomplished with a macro.

The first thing to do is to plan out the form to which you want the macro to expand. In this case, it has to include the logic for picking an expression at random from those provided. The expansion should look something like this:

```
(let [n (rand-int 2)]
      (if (zero? n) (println "A") (println "B")))
```

First, the macro needs to pick a random number between 0 and 1. Then, if the number is 0, it executes the first expression, otherwise the second.

The macro for this is fairly straightforward, given the syntax described:

```
(defmacro rand-expr [form1 form2]
   `(let [n# (rand-int 2)]
         (if (zero? n#) ~form1 ~form2)))
```

And, it works as expected, with the same expression sometimes evaluating **(println "A")** and sometimes **(println "B")**, never both.

```
user=> (rand-expr (println "A") (println "B"))
B
nil
user=> (rand-expr (println "A") (println "B"))
B
nil
user=> (rand-expr (println "A") (println "B"))
A
nil
```

Implementing a Macro with Variadic Arguments

Macros can take variable numbers of arguments. An example of this would be the preceding macro, but with the requirement that it randomly evaluate one of any number of expressions, rather than just one of two.

```
(rand-expr-multi (println "A") (println "B") (println "C"))
```

Creating a macro which takes a variable number of forms as "arguments" is easily done, the same way as it is for a function:

```
(defmacro rand-expr-multi [& forms] …)
```

What about the macro body? How to handle the variable number of arguments? Obviously, since you don't know how many there are, you can't just reference them by name and slot them into place in an **if** expression as was done in the first draft of **rand-expr**. You might be tempted to use something like the **nth** function to select a random expression from the list, but consider: At macro-expansion time, when you're building the structure, you don't have access to the random value. It has to be generated within the *expansion* at runtime. If you generate it at compile time, it will effectively become a constant. Without access to the random value at expansion-time, you need to list all the possible expressions as options in one of Clojure's more primitive control structures. Macro expansion is a process purely of code *transformation*—keeping that fact firmly in mind will help avoid a lot of confusion about what is available at expansion time as opposed to run time.

One viable solution would be to try and generate an expansion of something along these lines:

```
(let [ct (count <number of expressions>))]
    (case (rand-int ct)
        0 (println "A")
        1 (println "B")
        2 (println "C")))
```

The most succinct way is to use splicing unquote to splice in the list of forms that constitute the body of the **case**. Noticing that these forms are alternating indexes and expressions lets you use the **interleave** function to generate the list to splice in, which shortens the code considerably:

```
(defmacro rand-expr-multi [& exprs]
    `(let [ct# ~(count exprs)]
        (case (rand-int ct#)
            ~@(interleave (range (count exprs)) exprs))))
```

It generates the expected expansion:

```
user=> (macroexpand-1 '(rand-expr-multi (println "A") (println "B") (println "C")))
```

```
(clojure.core/let [ct__2188__auto__ 3]
    (clojure.core/case (clojure.core/rand-int ct__2188__auto__)
        0 (println "A")
        1 (println "B")
        2 (println "C")))
```

Upon testing, it works as expected:

```
user=> (rand-expr (println "A") (println "B"))
B
nil
user=> (rand-expr (println "A") (println "B"))
A
Nil
user=> (rand-expr (println "A") (println "B"))
C
nil
user=> (rand-expr (println "A") (println "B"))
B
nil
user=> (rand-expr (println "A") (println "B"))
B
nil
```

Implementing a Macro Using Recursion

Macros can also be applied recursively. As an example, consider a custom macro, ++, which can be used instead of +, and which automatically replaces multiargument addition expressions with nested binary expressions which perform slightly better in Clojure (see Chapter 14 for a more comprehensive discussion of this issue). In other words, it takes easy-to-read expressions such as (++ 1 2 3 4 5) and transforms them to slightly better performing, but more complex expressions like (+ 1 (+ 2 (+ 3 (+ 4 5)))).

Like recursive functions, recursive macros must have a base case at which they no longer recur, or else they will continue recursing forever and cause a stack overflow error, though at compile time instead of runtime. For the ++ macro, the base case is when it is passed only one or two arguments. In that scenario, it merely emits a standard + expression. When given three or more arguments, it applies itself recursively to its argument list, emitting an additional nested expression with each level of recursion.

It's easiest to look at the code:

```
(defmacro ++ [& exprs]
    (if (>= 2 (count exprs)
        `(+ ~@exprs)
        `(+ ~@(first exprs) (++ ~@(rest exprs)))))
```

It is very straightforward. There is one if condition, which differentiates between the base and recursive case. In the base case, it simply splices the provided expressions into a straightforward application of the + function. In the recursive case, it also creates a + function application and splices in the first expression as the first argument. For the second argument, it recursively inserts ++, splicing in the rest of the expressions as its arguments.

When the macro is expanded, the first layer is unwrapped and shows that it is correct, at least so far.

```
user=> (macroexpand '(++ 1 2 3 4))
(clojure.core/+ 1 (user/++ 2 3 4))
```

To see the entire recursive expansion, you can use Stuart Sierra's **clojure.walk** library, which is packaged with Clojure. It includes a **macroexpand-all** which, unlike **macroexpand** or **macroexpand-1**, does recursively expand all the macros it can find until there are none left. Importing and running **macroexpand-all** gives the complete, final expansion:

```
user=> (clojure.walk/macroexpand-all '(++ 1 2 3 4))
(clojure.core/+ 1 (clojure.core/+ 2 (clojure.core/+ 3 4)))
```

Actually using the macro shows it has the same semantics as +. It should be ever so slightly faster, as well, although the difference isn't detectable without an elaborate benchmark.

```
user=> (++ 1 2 3 4)
10
```

Using Macros to Create DSLs

One common use of macros is to generate custom DSLs. Using macros, a few simple, intuitive expressions can generate much more bulky, complex code without exposing it to the user.

The potential use for DSLs in Clojure is unlimited. Enclojure (the web framework for Clojure currently in vogue) allows the user to define web application paths and restful APIs using a simple, immediately understandable DSL syntax. Another Clojure project, Incanter, provides a DSL based on the R programming language that is incredibly succinct and useful for doing statistics and building charts.

Clojure's DSLs are particularly effective because there is no sharp distinction between an API and a DSL. Every well-designed Clojure API automatically ends up looking a lot like a DSL, and as Clojure programs get more complex they tend to evolve high-level functions and macros that are extremely easy to read.

The following macro demonstrates a very rudimentary Clojure DSL, one that uses Clojure expressions to build something very similar to XML (minus complexities such as attributes and namespaces).

The **xml** macro shown here is slightly different from the previous examples of macros; its expansion is a string, rather than a collection of forms. A macro is used instead of a function because the DSL works by overriding the normal processing of the provided forms, rendering them to a string instead of evaluating them. It isn't the best way to process XML in Clojure, by a long shot—for that, look at the **clojure.xml**, **clojure.zip**, and Stuart Sierra's **clojure.contrib.prxml** libraries. This is just a small, manageable example that will show some of the versatility that macros provide.

The input of the macro is just a series of nested forms. The forms don't have to resolve: they will be transformed into a string by the macro without ever being evaluated. The macro transforms input like this:

```
(xml
    (book
        (authors
            (author "Luke")
            (author "Stuart")))))
```

Into output like this:

```
<book><authors><author>Luke</author><author>Stuart</author></authors></book>
```

The code itself is as follows:

```
(defn xml-helper [form]
    (if (not (seq? form))
        (str form)
        (let [name (first form)
              children (rest form)]
            (str "<" name ">"
                 (apply str (map xml-helper children))
                 "</" name ">"))))

(defmacro xml [form]
    (xml-helper form))
```

The macro is very lightweight. It is passed a single form which it immediately passes off to a helper function. Macro helper functions are a common idiom. Often, as in this case, the macro itself doesn't do any work at all, but only serves to obtain the original form as a sequence. From there, functions can do all the actual work of transformation. When this is possible, it is usually desirable, since functions are often much easier to reason about than macros. Just remember, the function will be evaluated at compile time, as the macro is expanded, so it will not have access to the full runtime state of your program.

The helper function is a simple recursive function. The base case is when the provided form is a primitive (not a sequence). It simply returns it as a string. When the form is a sequence, it creates and returns an XML string, using the first item as the element name and the rest of the items as children which it processes recursively.

Running the macro shows that it is working:

```
user=> (xml (book (authors (author "Luke") (author "Stuart"))))
"<book><authors><author>Luke</author><author>Stuart</author></authors></book>"
```

From an XML processing perspective, it is terribly primitive and should not be used for any real work. As a demonstration of the power of macros, it is beautiful. The conversion from nested expressions to XML string happens at *compile time*. Because **xml** is a macro which returns a string, a program using it will actually "see" the **xml** expression as a string literal! The mini-XML DSL shown here is now an extension of the Clojure compiler itself.

Obviously such power can be abused, and it is possible to use macros to build incredibly obtuse and convoluted expressions. When used correctly, they provide nearly unlimited power to change the language to suit any need.

Summary

Through macros, Clojure provides powerful, elegant metaprogramming facilities. In Clojure, code and data are interchangeable, and macros are compile-time functions which emit data that becomes code.

Macros can either build code directly, or use syntax-quoting to template their output. They are hygienic, in that symbols bound by macros must use the auto gensym feature to avoid potential collisions with existing symbols.

Although they can add complexity to a program, when used judiciously macros provide the means to eliminate nearly all repeated and boilerplate code. They allow the developer to create language-level control structures and abstractions, extending the language exactly as needed to fit the problem domain. Tasteful and restrained use of macros, along with Clojure's other dynamic features such as first-class functions, allows developers to create custom DSLs, organically adapting their systems to fit a problem domain, rather than being forced to restate their problems just to meet the demands of an inflexible system.

CHAPTER 13

■ ■ ■

Datatypes and Protocols

Clojure is built on abstractions: sequences, references, macros, and so forth. However, most of those abstractions are implemented in Java, as classes and interfaces. It is difficult to add new abstractions to the language (for example, a queue data structure) without implementing them in Java.

Clojure 1.2 introduces several new features to make it easier to implement new abstractions directly in Clojure, while still taking full advantage of the performance optimizations in the Java platform. Datatypes and protocols are roughly analogous to Java's classes and interfaces, but they are more flexible.

■ **Note** As of this writing, Clojure 1.2 has not yet been released. Although the concepts will remain the same, there may be minor changes in naming or syntax from what we describe in this chapter.

Protocols

A *protocol* is a set of methods. The protocol has a name and an optional documentation string. Each method has a name, one or more argument vectors, and an optional documentation string. That's it! There are no implementations, no actual code.

Protocols are created with defprotocol:

```
(defprotocol MyProtocol
  "This is my new protocol"
  (method-one [x] "This is the first method.")
  (method-two ([x] [x y]) "The second method."))
```

If you were to execute this example in the namespace my.code, the following Vars would be created:

- my.code/MyProtocol: A protocol object.

- my.code/method-one: A function of one argument.

- my.code/method-two: A function of one or two arguments.

method-one and method-two are *polymorphic* functions, meaning they can have different implementations for different types of objects. You can call method-one or method-two immediately after defprotocol, but they will throw an exception because no implementations have been defined.

What *is* a protocol? It's a contract, a set of capabilities. An object or a datatype (described in the next section) can declare that it supports a particular protocol, meaning that it has implementations for the methods in that protocol.

Protocols As Interfaces

Conceptually, a protocol is similar to a Java interface. In fact, `defprotocol` creates a Java interface with the same methods. You can AOT-compile the Clojure source file containing `defprotocol` and use the interface in Java code. The Java interface will be in a package matching the namespace in which the protocol was defined. The package, interface, and method names will be adjusted to obey Java naming rules, such as replacing hyphens with underscores. Each method in the interface will have one argument fewer than the protocol method: that argument is the `this` pointer in Java. The previous example would create an interface matching the following Java code:

```
package my.code;

public interface MyProtocol {
    public Object method_one();
    public Object method_two(Object y);
}
```

There is one important difference between protocols and interfaces: protocols have no inheritance. You cannot create "subprotocols" like Java's subinterfaces.

Protocols are also similar to "mix-in" facilities provided by languages such as Ruby, with another important difference: protocols have no implementation. As a result, protocols never conflict with one another, unlike mix-ins.

Datatypes

Although Clojure is not, strictly-speaking, an object-oriented language, sometimes it is tempting to think in object-oriented terms when dealing with the real world. Most applications have many "records" of the same "type" with similar "fields."

Prior to Clojure 1.2, the standard way to handle records was to use maps. This worked, but did not permit any performance optimizations from reusing the same keys in many maps.

StructMaps were one solution, but they had several problems. StructMaps have a predefined set of keys, but no actual "type" that can be queried at runtime. They cannot be printed and read back as StructMaps. They cannot have primitive-typed fields, and they cannot match the performance of instance fields in plain old Java objects.

Clojure 1.2 introduces datatypes as a replacement for StructMaps. A *datatype* is a named record type, with a set of named fields that can implement protocols and interfaces. Datatypes are created with `defrecord`:

```
(defrecord name [fields...])
```

For example, a datatype might store an employee record with two fields, name and room number:

```
user> (defrecord Employee [name room])
```

In this example, `defrecord` creates a new class named `Employee` It has a default constructor that takes arguments matching the fields of the type, in the same order. You can construct an instance of the datatype by adding a dot to the end of its name.

```
user> (def emp (Employee. "John Smith" 304))
```

Datatype instances behave like Clojure maps. You can retrieve the fields of a datatyped object by using keywords as accessor functions:

```
user> (:name emp)
"John Smith"
user> (:room emp)
304
```

This is much faster than map lookups and even faster than StructMap accessor functions. Datatype instances also support the `assoc` and `dissoc` functions.

```
user=> (defrecord Scientist [name iq])
user.Scientist
user=> (def x (Scientist. "Albert Einstein" 190))
#'user/x
user=> (assoc x :name "Stephen Hawking")
#:user.Scientist{:name "Stephen Hawking", :iq 190}
```

You can even `assoc` additional fields that were not part of the original datatype, without changing the object's type.

```
user=> (assoc x :field "physics")
#:user.Scientist{:name "Albert Einstein", :iq 190, :field "physics"}
```

However, if you dissoc one of the original datatype keys, you get an ordinary map as the result.

```
user=> (dissoc x :iq)
{:name "Albert Einstein"}
```

Implementing Protocols and Interfaces

A datatype, by itself, just stores data. A protocol, by itself, doesn't do anything at all. Together they form a powerful abstraction. Once a protocol has been defined, it can be *extended* to support any datatype. We say the datatype *implements* the protocol. At that point, the protocol's methods can be called on instances of that datatype.

In-Line Methods

When creating a datatype with `defrecord`, you can supply method implementations for any number of protocols. The syntax is as follows:

```
(defrecord name [fields...]
  SomeProtocol
```

```
  (method-one [args] ... method body ...)
  (method-two [args] ... method body ...)
AnotherProtocol
  (method-three [args] ... method body ...))
```

You can chain any number of protocols and methods after the fields vector. Each method implementation has the same number of arguments as the corresponding protocol method. Fields of the instance are available as local variables in the method bodies, using the same names.

```
(defrecord name [x y z]
  SomeProtocol
  (method-one [args]
    ...do stuff with x, y, and z...))
```

These are the only locals available in the method bodies: defrecord does not close over its lexical scope like fn, proxy, or reify, which is described in the section "Reifying Anonymous Datatypes."

Extending Java Interfaces

Datatypes can also implement methods from Java interfaces. For example, you could implement the java.lang.Comparable interface, allowing your new datatype to support the Clojure compare function:

```
user> (defrecord Pair [x y]
        java.lang.Comparable
          (compareTo [this other]
            (let [result (compare x (:x other))]
              (if (zero? result)
                (compare y (:y other))
                result))))
#'user/Pair
user> (compare (Pair 1 2) (Pair 1 2))
0
user> (compare (Pair 1 3) (Pair 1 100))
-1
```

Note that the this argument, representing the object on which the method was called, must be explicitly included. This means that Clojure implementations of Java methods will have one more argument than appears in the Java method signature.

Since most of Clojure's core functions are defined to operate on interfaces, they can be extended to support new datatypes. Clojure defines too many interfaces to list here, but they can be found in the Clojure source code. Some examples are clojure.lang.Seqable and clojure.lang.Reversible for the seq and rseq functions, respectively. In a future release (2.0 or later), these interfaces will likely be redefined as protocols.

defrecord does not support Java class inheritance, so it cannot override methods of Java classes, even abstract classes. However, it does permit you to override methods of java.lang.Object such as hashCode, equals, and toString. Simply include java.lang.Object in the defrecord as if it were an interface. Clojure will generate good value-based implementations of the hashCode and equals methods, so it is rarely necessary to implement them yourself.

Java interfaces sometimes define *overloaded methods* with the same name but different argument types. If the methods have different numbers of arguments (arities), just define each arity as if it were a distinct method. (Do not use the multiple-arity syntax of fn.) If the methods have arguments of different types, add type tags (Chapter 8) to disambiguate them.

Datatypes As Classes

A datatype is equivalent to a Java class containing public final instance fields and implementing any number of interfaces. It does not extend any base class except java.lang.Object.

Unlike Java classes, a datatype is not required to provide implementations for every method of its protocols or interfaces. Methods lacking an implementation will throw an AbstractMethodError when called on instances of that datatype.

When AOT-compiled, defrecord will generate a Java class with the same name as the datatype and a package name matching the current namespace (subject to Java name rules, as with protocols). The generated class will have two constructors: one with just the fields as arguments and one with two extra arguments; a metadata map and a map of additional fields, either of which may be nil.

You cannot add additional constructors to a datatype, nor can you add methods that are not defined in a protocol or interface.

To optimize the memory usage of your datatype, you can add primitive type hints to the fields. You can also type-hint fields with class names; this will not affect memory usage (all pointers are the same size) but can prevent reflection warnings.

```
user> (defrecord Point [#^double x #^double y])
#'user/Point
user> (Point. 1 5)
#:Point{:x 1.0, :y 5.0}
```

Extending Protocols to Pre-Existing Types

Sometimes you may want to create a new protocol that operates on an existing datatype. Assume, for now, that you cannot modify the source code of the defrecord. You can still extend the protocol to support that datatype, using the extend function:

```
(extend DatatypeName
  SomeProtocol
    {:method-one (fn [x y] ...)
     :method-two existing-function}
  AnotherProtocol
    {...})
```

extend takes a datatype name followed by any number of protocol/method map pairs. A *method map* is an ordinary map from method names, given as keywords, to their implementations. The implementations can be anonymous functions created with fn or symbols naming existing functions.

Because extend is an ordinary function, all its arguments are evaluated. This means you could store a method map in a Var and reuse it to extend several datatypes, providing functionality very similar to mix-ins.

```
(def defaults
    {:method-one (fn [x y] ...)
     :method-two (fn [] ...)})
```

```
(extend DefaultType
  SomeProtocol
    defaults)
(extend AnotherType
  SomeProtocol
    (assoc defaults :method-two (fn ...)))
```

There are two convenience macros that simplify the extension syntax, extend-type and extend-protocol. Use extend-type when you want to implement several protocols for the same datatype; use extend-protocol when you want to implement the same protocol for several datatypes.

```
(extend-type DatatypeName
  SomeProtocol
    (method-one [x] ... method body ...)
    (method-two [x] ...)
  AnotherProtocol
    (method-three [x] ...))

(extend-protocol SomeProtocol
  SomeDatatype
    (method-one [x] ...)
    (method-two [x y] ...)
  AnotherType
    (method-one [x] ...)
    (method-two [x y] ...))
```

Methods added using extend and its associated macros are attached to the protocol, not the datatype itself. This makes them more flexible (they work on standard Java classes, described in the following section) but slightly less efficient than methods embedded directly within defrecord.

Extending Java Classes and Interfaces

Datatypes and protocols are a powerful abstraction, but often you have to deal with Java classes for which you do not have the source code. Java does not provide a way to add new interfaces to an existing class (known as *interface injection*), but Clojure protocols can be extended to support existing Java classes.

extend, extend-type, and extend-protocol all accept Java classes as "types." This works on interfaces, too. You can write (extend-type SomeInterface...) to extend a protocol to all classes that implement SomeInterface. This opens up the possibility of multiple inheritance of implementation, because a class can implement more than one interface; the result is currently undefined and should be avoided.

Reifying Anonymous Datatypes

Sometimes you need an object that implements certain protocols or interfaces, but you do not want to create a named datatype. Clojure 1.2 supports this with the reify macro:

```
(reify
  SomeProtocol
```

```
    (method-one [] ...)
    (method-two [y] ...)
  AnotherProtocol
    (method-three [] ...))
```

reify's syntax is very similar to defrecord without the fields vector. Also, like defrecord, reify can extend methods of Java interfaces and java.lang.Object.

Unlike defrecord, the method bodies of reify are lexical closures, like anonymous functions created with fn, so they can capture local variables:

```
user> (def thing (let [s "Capture me!"]
                    (reify java.lang.Object
                      (toString [] s))))
#'user/thing
user> (str thing)
"Capture me!"
```

Many situations that formerly required the use of proxy can be handled with reify. In those cases, reify will be faster and simpler than proxy. However, reify is limited to implementing interfaces; it cannot override base class methods like proxy.

Conceptually, reify fills the same role as *anonymous inner classes* in Java.

Working with Datatypes and Protocols

Datatypes and protocols are a significant new feature in Clojure, and they will have a major impact on how most Clojure programs are written. Standards and best practices are still developing, but a few guidelines have emerged:

- Prefer reify to proxy unless you need to override base class methods.

- Prefer defrecord to gen-class unless you need gen-class features for Java interoperability.

- Prefer defrecord to defstruct in all cases.

- Specify your abstractions as protocols, not interfaces.

- Prefer protocols to multimethods for the case of single-argument type-based dispatch.

- Add type hints only where necessary for disambiguation or performance (Chapter 14); most types will be inferred automatically.

Datatypes and protocols do not remove any existing features: defstruct, gen-class, proxy, and multimethods are all still there. Only defstruct is likely to be deprecated.

The major difference between Java classes and protocols/datatypes is the lack of inheritance. The protocol extension mechanism is designed to enable method reuse *without* concrete inheritance and its associated problems.

A Complete Example

Here's a version of the classic "payroll" example using protocols and datatypes. Your payroll system will have one method that calculates employees' monthly paychecks based on how many hours they work:

```
(defprotocol Payroll
  (paycheck [emp hrs]))
```

Then there are two kinds of employees: "hourly" employees who are paid by the hour and "salaried" employees who are paid a fixed portion of their annual salary each month, regardless of how many hours they work:

```
(defrecord HourlyEmployee [name rate]
  Payroll
  (paycheck [hrs] (* rate hrs)))

(defrecord SalariedEmployee [name salary]
  Payroll
  (paycheck [hrs] (/ salary 12.0)))
```

Notice that you have not defined an IS-A relationship. There is no "Employee" base type; none is needed. All you have said is: these two types exist, and both support the paycheck method of Payroll.
    Now you can define a couple of employees and calculate their paychecks:

```
user=> (def emp1 (HourlyEmployee. "Devin" 12))
user=> (def emp2 (SalariedEmployee. "Casey" 30000))
user=> (paycheck emp1 105)
1260
user=> (paycheck emp2 120)
2500.0
```

You might also need to send paychecks to contractors: in that case, the contractor's payment is specified before they start working. This could be another datatype, but you can also implement it using reify:

```
(defn contract [amount]
  (reify Payroll (paycheck [hrs] amount)))
```

As shown in the following example:

```
user=> (def con1 (contract 5000))
user=> (paycheck con1 80)
5000
```

Advanced Datatypes

Datatypes defined with defrecord are useful for storing structured data, but fundamentally they always act like maps. If you want to define a completely new type, one that doesn't behave like a map, use the deftype macro instead. deftype is a "lower-level" version of defrecord.

```
(deftype name [fields...]
  SomeProtocol
    (some-method [this x y] ...)
  SomeInterface
    (aMethod [this] ...))
```

The syntax is the same as `defrecord`, but `deftype` will not create any default method implementations for you. You must suppply all the method implementations, even standard Object methods such as `equals` and `hashCode`. `deftype` creates a "bare" Java class; it is intended to allow the redefinition of core data structures, such as vectors or maps, in Clojure itself.

Summary

Datatypes and protocols are two of the most exciting new features planned for Clojure 1.2. They provide a powerful solution to many of the same problems that object-oriented programming was intended to solve, but without the baggage of implementation inheritance. In fact, datatypes and protocols bear a remarkable similarity to early research in object-oriented design. They elegantly handle the problem of adding new functions to existing types, sometimes called the "expression problem." Because they are built on the Java platform's heavily-optimized method dispatch, they also provide excellent performance.

CHAPTER 14

∎∎∎

Performance

In principle, Clojure can be just as fast as Java: both are compiled to Java bytecode instructions, which are executed by a Java Virtual Machine. Clojure's design is careful to avoid features—such as continuations or a Common Lisp-like condition system—that would severely compromise performance on the JVM. But Clojure is still a young language, and has not had the benefit of hundreds of thousands of programmer-hours spent optimizing the compiler. As a result, Clojure code will generally run slower than equivalent Java code. However, with some minor adjustments, Clojure performance can usually be brought near Java performance. Don't forget that Java is always available as a fallback for performance-critical sections of code.

Profiling on the JVM

The number one rule when evaluating performance of any programming language or algorithm is: test! Do not assume that one technique will necessarily be faster because it appears to have fewer steps or use fewer variables. This is especially true on modern JVMs such as Hotspot, which constantly measure code performance and dynamically recompile critical sections while your application is running.

So-called *microbenchmarks* that measure a single operation in isolation are meaningless in this environment. Also meaningless are benchmarks where the start-up time of the JVM dominates the measurement (this is a frequent error in comparisons between Java and C++). Modern JVMs are typically optimized for throughput, maximizing the total number of operations that can be performed over a long period of time.

General Tips for Java Performance

Java Virtual Machines have a number of options that affect performance. First, for JVMs that distinguish between "client" and "server" modes, the "server" mode will always offer better overall performance (at the expense of longer start-up time).

Second, the size of the Java heap space and the choice of garbage collection strategy impact performance. This is especially true for Clojure, which because of its use of immutable data, tends to use more heap space and put more stress on the garbage collector than Java.

There are many more tuning parameters in modern JVMs that can affect performance. Make sure you are familiar with the "knobs" offered by your VM and experiment to see how they affect your particular application.

Simple Profiling with Time

Clojure has a very simple profiling tool built-in, the **time** macro. **time** takes a single expression, evaluates it, and prints how long it took in milliseconds:

```
user=> (time (reduce + (range 100)))
"Elapsed time: 1.005 msecs"
4950
```

As previously noted, such microbenchmarks are all but meaningless in the context of the JVM. A slightly better measurement can be obtained by repeating the same calculation thousands of times in a tight loop:

```
user=> (time (dotimes [i 100000]
                (reduce + (range 100))))
"Elapsed time: 252.594 msecs"
nil
```

However, this still does not present the whole picture, as the JVM might reoptimize the calculation between executions of the loop. A more accurate result can be obtained by repeating the loop several times:

```
user=> (dotimes [j 5]
          (time (dotimes [i 100000]
                  (reduce + (range 100)))))
"Elapsed time: 355.759 msecs"
"Elapsed time: 239.404 msecs"
"Elapsed time: 217.362 msecs"
"Elapsed time: 221.168 msecs"
"Elapsed time: 217.753 msecs"
```

As you can see, in this example, the time bounces around for a couple of iterations before converging around 220 milliseconds. This pattern is typical of the JVM.

However, even with this information, you cannot predict exactly how the calculation **(reduce + (range 100))** will perform in the context of a large application. Only further testing will tell.

Also, be aware of the impact of lazy sequences. If the expression you are testing uses lazy sequences (for example, using **map**), the **time** macro may only report the time to initialize the sequence. To measure the time to realize the entire sequence, you must use **doall**, which can be difficult to do in a complex data structure and is probably not representative of how the structure will actually be used.

Using Java Profiling Tools

Since Clojure compiles to Java bytecode, Java profiling tools will work on Clojure, but a discussion of such tools is outside the scope of this book.

The best rule-of-thumb is this: write your code in the simplest, most direct way possible, then test to see if it meets your performance expectations. If it does not, use profiling tools to identify the critical sections that matter most to performance, and tweak or rewrite those sections until they meet your performance goals. The following pages describe some techniques for optimizing critical sections of Clojure code.

Memoization

One simple technique for speeding up large, complex functions is *memoization*, which is a form of caching. Each time it is called, a memoized function will store its return value in a table, along with the input arguments. If that function is called again with the same arguments, it can return the value stored in the table without repeating the calculation.

Clojure has built-in support for memoization with the **memoize** function, which takes a function as its argument and returns a memoized version of that function.

```
(defn really-slow-function [x y z] ...)
(def faster-function (memoize really-slow-function))
```

Memoization is a classic example of trading increased memory usage for faster execution time. If a function takes longer to calculate its result than a hash table lookup, and it will be called frequently with the same inputs, it is a good candidate for memoization. Only *pure* functions—that is, functions that always return the same output for a particular input—can be memoized.

Reflection and Type Hints

As you know, Java is a *statically typed* language: it knows the types of all objects at compile time. Clojure is *dynamically typed*, meaning the types of some objects may not be known until runtime.

To implement dynamically-typed function calls on top of statically-typed Java, Clojure uses a Java feature called *reflection*. Reflection allows code to inspect Java classes at runtime and call methods by name. However, reflective method calls are much slower than compiled method calls.

Clojure allows you to add *type hints* to symbols and expressions to help the compiler avoid reflective method calls. Type hints are indicated through read-time metadata (see Chapter 8) using the **:tag** keyword. A type-hinted symbol would be written as **#^{:tag hint} symbol**, this is usually abbreviated as **#^hint symbol**. The type hint is a Java class name. (The class name may also be a string, which is only rarely needed to handle obscure Java interoperability problems.)

To find out whether a method call is reflective or not, set the compiler flag ***warn-on-reflection*** to true. After that, evaluating any code that contains a reflective call will cause the Clojure compiler to print a warning message.

```
user=> (set! *warn-on-reflection* true)
true
user=> (defn nth-char [s n]
         (.charAt s n))
Reflection warning - call to charAt can't be resolved.
```

The warning can usually be eliminated by adding a type hint to the symbol on which you are calling the method. This works for both function parameters and locals bound with **let**.

```
;; No reflection warnings:
user=> (defn nth-char [#^String s n]
         (.charAt s n))
#'user/nth-char
user=> (defn nth-char [s n]
         (let [#^String st s]
```

```
      (.charAt st n)))
#'user/nth-char
```

In the case of Java methods overloaded on different argument types, further type hints may be needed. For example, the **String.replace** method accepts either **char** or **CharSequence** arguments. You have to type hint all three arguments to avoid reflection.

```
user=> (defn str-replace [#^String s a b]
          (.replace s a b))
Reflection warning - call to replace can't be resolved.
#'user/str-replace
user=> (defn str-replace [#^String s
                          #^CharSequence a
                          #^CharSequence b]
          (.replace s a b))
#'user/str-replace
```

Note that type hints are not type *coercions*, they cannot convert one type into another. Calling a type-hinted method with the wrong types will result in a runtime error:

```
user=> (str-replace "Hello" \H \J)
java.lang.ClassCastException: java.lang.Character cannot
be cast to java.lang.CharSequence
```

Also, note that *incorrect* type hints will cause a reflection warning:

```
user=> (defn str-replace [#^String s #^Integer a #^Integer b]
          (.replace s a b))
Reflection warning - call to replace can't be resolved.
#'user/str-replace
```

You can type-hint the return value of a function by adding a type tag to its Var when it is defined. This works for any Var, such as those used as global values.

```
user=> (defn greeting [] "Hello, World!")  ;; no type hint
#'user/greeting
user=> (.length (greeting))
Reflection warning - reference to field length can't be resolved.
13
user=> (defn #^String greeting [] "Hello, World!")
#'user/greeting
user=> (.length (greeting))  ;; no reflection warning
13
user=> (defn greeting {:tag String} [] "Hello, World!") ;; same as above
```

In rare cases, type hinting symbols will not be sufficient to avoid reflection. In that case, you can type-hint an entire expression:

```
user=> (.length (identity "Hello, World!"))
Reflection warning - reference to field length can't be resolved.
13
```

```
user=> (.length #^String (identity "Hello, World!"))
13
```

The Clojure compiler is pretty clever about tracking the types of objects. For example, the return types of Java methods are always known and never need to be hinted. Given just a few hints, the compiler can usually *infer* most of the other type information it needs. In general, you should write your code first without any type hints, then set ***warn-on-reflection*** and add them only where necessary for performance.

Working with Primitives

Java's type system is not 100% object-oriented; it supports the *primitive* types **boolean**, **char**, **byte**, **short**, **int**, **long**, **float**, and **double**. These primitive types do not fit into the standard Java class hierarchy. When used with methods that expect an Object, primitives must be *boxed* in the classes Boolean, Character, Byte, Short, Integer, Long, Float, and Double. Starting with Java 1.5, the Java compiler automatically boxes and unboxes primitives as needed.

In Clojure, everything is an Object, so numbers are always boxed. This can be seen by inspecting the results of simple arithmetic:

```
user=> (class (+ 1 1))
java.lang.Integer
```

However, in the JVM, operations on boxed numbers are slower than operations on unboxed primitives. So for math-intensive applications, Clojure code with boxed numbers will be slower than Java code that works directly with primitives.

Loop Primitives

Clojure supports primitive types where it matters most: in the body of a loop. In the bindings vector of **loop** (or **let**) you can coerce values to primitive types with the functions **boolean**, **char**, **byte**, **short**, **int**, **float**, and **double**. Here is an example of Euclid's algorithm for computing the greatest common denominator of two integers:

```
(defn gcd [a b]
  (loop [a (int a), b (int b)]
    (cond (zero? a) b
          (zero? b) a
          (> a b) (recur (- a b) b)
          :else (recur a (- b a)))))
```

The primitive coercions to **int** happen in the initialization vector of the loop. This version is about twelve times faster than the non-primitive version. But, be careful! Suppose you had chosen to implement the same algorithm using the **mod** (modulo) function. That code would be *slower* using primitives, because arguments to Clojure functions (except arithmetic) are always boxed. Therefore, when using loop primitives, you should only call the following *primitive-aware* functions:

- Arithmetic functions **+**, **-**, *****, and **/**

- Comparison functions **==**, **<**, **>**, **<=**, and **>=**

- Predicate functions **pos?**, **neg?**, and **zero?**

- Java methods with primitive argument and return types

- Unchecked arithmetic functions (described in the following section)

Notice that the general-purpose = function is not on this list. Instead, use the == function, which only works on numbers. Full primitive support for all Clojure functions, including user-defined functions, is planned for a future release.

Numeric literals must also be coerced to primitive types to use primitive operations. For example, the following code computes the sum of the integers from 1 to 100:

```
(let [max (int 100)]
  (loop [sum (int 0)
         i (int 1)]
    (if (> i max)
      sum
      (recur (+ sum i) (inc i)))))
```

The initial values of the loop variables **sum** and **i** must be coerced into primitives with **int**. The primitive coercion of **max** is outside the loop because it only needs to be done once. If you used the literal number 100 instead of the local variable **max**, the code would still work, but it would not be quite as fast.

Unchecked Integer Arithmetic

Clojure's primitive arithmetic operations are defined to be *safe*, meaning they will throw an error if the result of an operation is too big for the result type. For example, this loop, designed to calculate 2^{64}, throws an exception:

```
user=> (let [max (int 64)
             two (int 2)]
         (loop [total (int 1), n (int 0)]
           (if (== n max)
             total
             (recur (* total two) (inc n)))))
java.lang.ArithmeticException: integer overflow
```

However, there are certain algorithms (such as hashing) where the silent overflow behavior of integer arithmetic is desirable. For these cases, Clojure provides a set of functions that perform integer arithmetic exactly like Java's arithmetic operators. They all accept Integer or Long arguments, and are primitive-aware.

The following functions are subject to integer overflow: **unchecked-add**, **unchecked-subtract**, **unchecked-multiply**, **unchecked-negate**, **unchecked-inc**, and **unchecked-dec**.

```
user=> (unchecked-inc Integer/MAX_VALUE)
-2147483648
user=> (unchecked-negate Integer/MIN_VALUE)
-2147483648
```

The **unchecked-divide** and **unchecked-remainder** functions are subject to lossy truncation.

```
user=> (unchecked-divide 403 100)
4
```

The unchecked operations will be slightly faster than the standard arithmetic functions when used with loop primitives. However, make certain you can accept the loss of safety before switching to unchecked arithmetic.

Primitive Arrays

Starting with Clojure 1.1, you can type-hint arrays of primitives: Java **boolean[]**, **char[]**, **byte[]**, **short[]**, **int[]**, **long[]**, **float[]**, and **double[]** can be hinted as **#^booleans**, **#^chars**, **#^bytes**, **#^shorts**, **#^ints**, **#^longs**, **#^floats**, and **#^doubles**, respectively. (There is also **#^objects** for **Object[]**.)

Type-hinted arrays support primitive operations using **aget** and **aset**. There is no need to use the type-specific setter functions such as **aset-int** and **aset-double**; in fact, those functions will be slower than **aset** for type-hinted primitive arrays. For **aset**, the new value must also be the correct primitive type. For both **aget** and **aset**, the array index must be a primitive **int**. The **amap** and **areduce** macros (described in Chapter 10) are an excellent way to perform fast operations on primitive arrays while retaining a functional style.

Transients

As you know by now, all of Clojure's built-in data structures are *immutable* and *persistent* to ensure safe concurrent access from multiple threads. But what if you have a data structure that you know will only be used by a single thread? Should you still have to pay the immutable/persistent performance penalty? Clojure's answer is: No!

Clojure 1.1 introduced *transients*, temporary mutable data structures, as a performance optimization. They are useful when you are building up a large data structure through a series of steps.

The key feature of transients is that they do not change the functional style of your code. Importantly, they do *not* give you a truly mutable data structure (like Java's collection classes) that you can bash at with imperative code. The mutable nature of transients is largely an implementation detail.

Transients are best explained by an example. The following code creates a map from ASCII characters to their decimal values:

```
(loop [m {}, i 0]
  (if (> i 127)
    m
    (recur (assoc m (char i) i) (inc i))))
```

Here is the same loop using transients:

```
(loop [m (transient {}), i 0]
  (if (> i 127)
    (persistent! m)
    (recur (assoc! m (char i) i) (inc i))))
```

Notice that very little changes. This example shows the three code modifications required to use transients:

1. Initialize a transient version of the data structure with the **transient** function. Vectors, hash maps, and hash sets are supported.

2. Replace all uses of **conj**, **assoc**, **dissoc**, **disj**, and **pop** with their transient versions: **conj!**, **assoc!**, **dissoc!**, **disj!**, and **pop!**.

3. Call **persistent!** on the result to return a normal persistent data structure.

One important feature of transients is that the **transient** and **persistent!** functions run in constant time, regardless of the size of the input. Therefore, it is very efficient to call **transient** on a large data structure, manipulate it using transient-specific functions, and then call **persistent!** before returning the structure.

Remember, transients are *not* mutable data structures like Java collections. Just like persistent data structures, you must use the *return value* of any function that modifies the structure. The following imperative-style code will not work:

```
;; bad code!
(let [m (transient {})]
  (dotimes [i 127]
    (assoc! m (char i) i))
  (persistent! m))
```

The **dotimes** macro creates an imperative loop; on each iteration, the return value of **assoc!** is discarded. The exact results of this code are unpredictable, but always wrong.

Generally, transients are used within a single function or loop/recur block. They *can* be passed around to other functions, but they impose several restrictions:

*   Thread isolation is enforced. Accessing the transient structure from another thread will throw an exception.

*   After calling **persistent!**, the transient version of the structure is gone. Attempts to access it will throw an exception.

*   Intermediate versions of the transient structure cannot be stored or used; only the latest version is available (unlike persistent data structures).

The advantage to transients is that their modifying operations are much faster than those of persistent data structures. In general, anywhere you are building up a large data structure recursively, transients will offer a performance boost. But use of transients should almost always be limited to the body of a single function, not spread across different sections of code.

Var Lookups

Every time you use a Var, Clojure has to look up the Var's value. If you are repeatedly using the same Var in a loop, those lookups can slow down the code. To avoid this performance penalty, use **let** to bind the Var's value to a local for the duration of the loop, as in this example:

```
(def *var* 100)
(let [value *var*]
  ... loop using value instead of *var* ...)
```

Use this technique with caution: it does not always yield a performance improvement and may become unnecessary in a future Clojure release.

Inlining

Inlining—replacing a function call with the compiled body of the function—is a common optimization technique in compilers. The Hotspot JVM does extensive inlining of performance-critical code.

Clojure automatically inlines operations on primitives. However, arithmetic functions that take a variable number of arguments, such as **+**, will only be inlined in the two-argument case. That means this code:

```
(+ a b c d)
```

will be faster when written as:

```
(+ a (+ b (+ c d)))
```

especially when the values involved are primitives. This may also become unnecessary in a future release.

Macros and definline

In a sense, macros are a kind of inlining, because they are expanded at compile time. However, macros cannot be used as arguments to higher-order functions like **map** and **reduce**.

As an alternative, Clojure offers the **definline** form. **definline** looks, and works, like **defmacro**: its body should return a data structure representing the code to be compiled. Unlike **defmacro**, it creates a real function that can be used anywhere a normal function can. Here's an example.

```
;; a normal function:
(defn square [x] (* x x))
;; an inlined function:
(definline square2 [x] `(* ~x ~x))
```

definline is labeled "experimental" in Clojure. It exists primarily to work around the problem that functions cannot receive primitive arguments or return primitive values. When that feature is added, the JVM will do the inlining for you and **definline** will be unnecessary.

Summary

As Donald Knuth famously said, "Premature optimization is the root of all evil." The key word is *premature*. Trying to optimize a function before you have tested it is pointless. Trying to optimize an application before you have identified the performance-critical sections is worse than useless. In a just-in-time compiled, self-optimizing runtime such as the JVM, the situation is even more precarious, because it is difficult to look at a piece of code and predict how fast it will run.

The best approach is to step back and consider performance from two different angles. First, high-level performance considerations, such as avoiding bottlenecks or unnecessary I/O, should be considered during the design phase of an application. Low-level performance optimizations should be postponed until after the first draft of the code, when performance-critical sections can be identified through profiling.

Clojure provides many tools to optimize code without sacrificing its functional style. When those tools are insufficient, you can always fall back on imperative programming techniques, either in Clojure code (using arrays) or by writing Java code and calling it from Clojure.

Index

J

K